HOW to BE the **HEAD**
and
NOT the **TAIL!**

Dessie,

May you continue to stir up the gift of God in you & be "The Head" in all your endeavors as God has preordained for you since the beginning of time.

Stay Blessed!

Tony

HOW to BE the **HEAD**
and
NOT the **TAIL!**

A Christian Manifesto
for Making Six Figures

C. Joyce Farrar-Rosemon

Providence House Publishers
PROVIDENCE PUBLISHING CORPORATION
FRANKLIN, TENNESSEE

Printed in the United States of America

09   08   07   06   05   1   2   3   4   5

Library of Congress Control Number: 2005902507

ISBN: 1-57736-333-7

Cover design by Hope Seth and Joey McNair

The illustration on p. 26 is from *What Treasure Mapping Can Do for You* by Mary Katherine MacDougall © 1968 by Unity School of Christianity. Used by permission.

Scripture quotations, unless noted otherwise, are taken from the HOLY BIBLE, King James Version, Cambridge, 1769.

Scripture references marked (NIV) are taken from the LIFE APPLICATION BIBLE, NIV. Copyright © 2000 by The Zondervan Corporation/NIV 1973, 1978, 1984 by International Bible Society, 1988, 1989, 1990, 1991, 1993, 1996, 2000 by Tyndale House Publishers, Inc. All rights reserved. Used by permission of The Zondervan Corporation.

PROVIDENCE HOUSE PUBLISHERS
an imprint of
Providence Publishing Corporation
238 Seaboard Lane • Franklin, Tennessee 37067
www.providence-publishing.com
800-321-5692

I would like to express my thanks
to the late Mama Emma Jones of Jesus Christ Center of Truth
in Atlanta, Georgia, for believing in my dream,
for telling me Sunday after Sunday that I could do it.
Thank you for holding my hand while I went through
my spiritual labor pains. Thank you, Mama Emma, for telling me
repeatedly with that smile and laugh and certainty
that only you could convey, that I was "Trump material."

CONTENTS

ACKNOWLEDGMENTS

I wish to extend a heartfelt thanks to my husband,
Tillmon H. Rosemon Jr., for believing in and
supporting my vision to be a broker.

A special thank you to my loving miracle child David
who understood and gave Mom time to write her book.

And to God who daily loads me with benefits,
how can I adequately thank You for showing me
how to be the Head and not the Tail?
Thank You for the experience of life, for Your
wondrous creation of the earth and each sunrise.
You are truly amazing!

INTRODUCTION

The idea for this self-help book came about from my desire to share my experiences as they related to my success in real estate sales during a year in which I experienced several tragedies. By mid-2001, I experienced two legal threats against my real estate license (which is my livelihood) and the threat of dissolution of my real estate company. During the week of September 11, 2001, my dad was diagnosed with terminal prostate cancer. On Christmas morning 2001, at 6:30 A.M., my dad suffered a cardiac arrest and was pronounced dead at the hospital one hour later.

Following my dad's death, I was left to find a personal care home for my then fifty-three-year-old disabled brother and a nursing home for my eighty-two-year-old mother who was in the advanced stages of Alzheimer's disease. Days after my dad's death, my fifty-six-year-old eldest brother was committed to a psychiatric hospital after attempting to burn down our parents' house. The idea came to me to write this book when, from all appearances, there was no way I could achieve a six-figure income. I questioned the wisdom of writing this book until I had actually made six figures myself. My inner spirit prompted me to write it, so I did.

In spite of the depression, hardships, misunderstandings, accusations, the loss of Dad, time at work and away from my immediate family, by the end of 2001, I had unknowingly made six figures in sales. What is remarkable about this accomplishment was that I wasn't trying to make it happen; I didn't have the desire, energy, or a plan. I wasn't even thinking about it happening. Bear in mind, I was caught up in caring for my then six-year-old son, supervising my twenty-four real estate agents, caring for my mother and disabled brothers, and trying to be a good wife. My plate was full, and on some days, I was totally exhausted. All I could do was take it one day—one hour—at a time and simply do what was set before me and pray. The verse, "watch and pray," took on a new, literal, and active meaning for me.

I decided to subtitle this book a "Christian Manifesto" because I wanted it to be a public declaration of the Christian principles and policies I used to become a broker of a highly successful real estate firm in metropolitan Atlanta. I wanted to share how I—with my husband's and God's help, during my seventh month of pregnancy, and with ten dollars in the operating account—opened a firm in 1992 that by 2001 boasted a staff of twenty-four agents and that had gross sales and contracts exceeding seventeen million dollars.

In this book I share how I turned crises into breakthroughs. This book details how I went from one level to the next: a sort of climbing-Jacob's-ladder type of experience. This book shows readers how you go from glory to glory. It lays out how you go from one sale to the next sale, from being a sales agent to being a broker co-owner, from leasing space to owning the building. This book is a response to an often-heard theme preached from various pulpits across America, Sunday after Sunday, exhorting Christian believers to be "the head and not the tail." This is an interactive book that shows and details a step-by-step process for readers on how to be "the head and *not the tail.*"

The questions that I set out to answer in this book are: How do we do it? How do we as Christian believers become more than conquerors? How do we possess the land? How will the riches of the world be turned over to us? How does the average Jane Doe or John Doe become a millionaire or, at the least, achieve a six-figure income?

Another way to pose these questions is to ask, "How can I, in my secular job, inherit the riches of this world and become successful and prosperous? Must I become an ordained minister or will God give me this inheritance as a carpet cleaner, hairdresser, teacher, lawyer, doctor, or as in my chosen profession, a real estate agent? Is the path to riches perhaps best accomplished through working for corporate America, investing in stocks and bonds, oil, technology, or investing overseas?" These are the questions I have set out to answer.

In this book I delineate the successful application of the Christian principles I used. I give a spiritual interpretation of the promises of God in His Word and show how they undergird the steps I take in my life and in the lives of the real estate agents I manage each day.

I don't claim to be Pollyanna in my views throughout this book. I am well aware that there are many non-Christians who are successful and many of them are millionaires. God is a good God. In Matthew 5:45 it expains, ". . . for he maketh his sun to rise on the evil and on the good and he sendeth rain on the just and on the unjust." As the healed man in John 9:25–27 who was blind from birth retorted to his skeptics, ". . . whereas I was blind, now I see." I, too, can only say, whereas I was lost and blind, I now see. My success continues to accelerate and it is undaunting. I am at the point in my life where I can say, as in Deuteronomy 28:2, that the blessings of God now pursue and overtake me. This book chronicles certain events in my life that I can only explain as supernatural, which demonstrate the favor, the anointing of God, in my life.

I have been licensed in real estate since 1983, and have been a life member of the Million Dollar Club since 1990. Annually across the U.S. many individuals seek to secure their pots of gold by obtaining their real estate licenses. Unfortunately, quite a few find out in a hurry that sales is not for the faint of heart. The National Association of Realtors reported in the June 2002 issue of *Realtor Magazine* that the 2001 national, median income for agents with less than five years of experience was only twenty thousand dollars. Although one can obtain a six-figure income as a nonbeliever, my experience as a born-again Christian is that it has only been through God's miraculous power that I have been propelled to the prominent position I have achieved thus far. My justification for such views can be traced back to prophecy; dreams; Bible passages; His still, small voice; and individuals who have prompted me along the road to success.

What follows is my attempt to show the step-by-step process I took to achieve my success. But it is more important to show that this process has no respect to time, place, educational level, age, gender, or race. I am confident that the methods that I have outlined in this book will work effectively in the drug-infested inner cities of America (I grew up in one), the apartheid-torn country of South Africa, or in the ghettos of Russia. *This is my gift to the body of Christ.* My prayer is that readers will take these spiritual truths and business principles and not just increase their livelihood, but more important, increase the body of Christ by becoming fishers of men and women who have been bruised by life's adversities.

HOW to BE the HEAD
and
NOT the TAIL!

Chapter 1

Is Your Heart in Your Work?

And the Lord shall make thee the head, and not the tail; and thou shalt be above only, and thou shalt not be beneath; if that thou hearken unto the commandments of the Lord thy God, which I command thee this day, to observe and to do them (Deut. 28:13).

For it is he that giveth thee the power to get wealth (Deut. 8:18).

Before starting off in sales or your employment venture, it's important to determine whether you have what it takes to be successful in the long run. First of all, it is important to define what the word "sales" means. We are all involved in sales whether we choose to be or not. Life is all about sales, whether we call ourselves salespersons or not. Employees are paid salespersons and the CEO can either be an independent contractor or a paid employee. Both are selling a product, be it cheeseburgers, software, soft drinks, encyclopedias, real estate, or cleaning supplies.

Webster's dictionary defines the word "sale(s)" as the "transfer of ownership of property from one person to another in return for money." My working definition, and the one I will use throughout this book, is as follows: "the ability to influence someone else to make a decision in your favor to obtain the service(s) you are promoting in exchange for something of value." Examples of this would be a person's decision to buy a house, a set of encyclopedias, or an insurance policy, or even a decision to give one's life to Christ.

With this definition in place, it's important to establish whether or not you have a heart for sales. Are you cut out to sell houses, encyclopedias, insurance, or the gospel? What you need is an honest self-analysis—what do you enjoy doing? Would you do it without getting paid for it? Ask for guidance; what is the desire in your heart, what is your passion? Are you in it for the money, the fame, or the acclaim of others?

Regardless of your profession, according to the previous defini-tion and to the Scriptures referenced at the beginning of this chapter, the modern-day Church should contain a powerhouse of individuals who demonstrate the prosperity of God in their lives, as reflected in health, wealth, and loving family relationships. Their countenances should be bright, and there should be something special or glorious about them, like Stephen in Acts 6:15, "they saw that his face was like the face of an angel."

How does the modern-day Church empower its congregation? To answer this, I refer to the classic story on prosperity that is told in 2 Kings 4:1–7:

> Now there cried a certain woman of the wives of the sons of the prophets unto Elisha saying, Thy servant my husband is dead; and thou knowest that thy servant did fear the Lord; and the creditor is come to take unto him my two sons to be bondmen. And Elisha said unto her, What shall I do for thee? Tell me, what hast thou in the house? And she said, Thine handmaid hath not any thing in the house, save a pot of oil. Then he said, Go, borrow thee vessels abroad of all thy neighbors, even empty vessels, borrow not a few. And when thou art come in, thou shalt shut the door upon thee and upon thy sons, and shalt pour out into all those vessels, and thou shalt set aside that which is full. So she went from him, and shut the door upon her and upon her sons, who brought the vessels to her; and she poured out. And it came to pass, when the vessels were full, that she said unto her son, Bring me yet a vessel. And he said unto her, There is not a vessel more. And the oil stayed. Then she came and told the man of God.

And he said, Go, sell the oil, and pay the debt, and live thou and thy children of the rest.

Do we read this story as a historical account or do we interpret that since God is the same yesterday, today, and tomorrow, there must be some spiritual truths contained in this allegory? If the answer is yes to the latter, then the relevancy of this story for the modern-day believer is that the modern-day prophet should empower them to use what they have—that is, their talents that lie within them—to prosper.

The exchange of first fruits, i.e., the giving of tithes and offerings (Mal. 3:8–12), should render a blessing that shows the recipients how to go within themselves and pull out their talents. Like the widow in 2 Kings 4, the exchange should produce food every day for the individual and her family. Through this exchange, Elisha showed the woman a method of obtaining wealth, a system of exchange, a livelihood that she could use to take care of her family, and also a life skill, a job that her children could participate in after she had died.

Not only does the exchange produce blessings in the natural (food every day), but also in the supernatural or the miraculous, as when the one pot of oil multiplied itself and did not run out until all the vessels were filled. The exchange should, number one, deal with fear. Secondly, it should deal with what you have, as well as your strengths and weaknesses. In a time of famine, what little you have will not be used up. Nor will your sons, your inheritance, perish. It should produce favor in your life so that supernatural blessings occur. "A thousand shall fall at your side, and ten thousand at your right hand, but it shall not come nigh thee" (Ps. 91:7). Not only in the natural will your supply not be used up, but in the spiritual as well.

This means that supernaturally you will have enough oil (like the five wise virgins in Matthew 25:1–13) to enable you to overcome any obstacle in this natural world and be prepared to meet the groom, which is Jesus Christ, in the next heavenly realm. It is important enough that I feel I must share with you this parable so that its spiritual meaning is totally understood. Please note that my attempt is not to load the reader with a lot of Scriptures, but to give understanding and wisdom. The passage from Matthew 25 is as follows:

> Then shall the kingdom of heaven be likened unto ten virgins, which took their lamps, and went forth to meet the bridegroom. And five of them were wise, and five were foolish. They that were foolish took their lamps, and took no oil with them: But the wise took oil in their vessels with their lamps. While the bridegroom tarried, they all slumbered and slept. And at midnight there was a cry made, Behold, the bridegroom cometh; go ye out to meet him. Then all those virgins arose, and trimmed their lamps. And the foolish said unto the wise, Give us of your oil; for our lamps are gone out. But the wise answered, saying, Not so; lest there be not enough for us and you: but go ye rather to them that sell, and buy for yourselves. And while they went to buy, the bridegroom came; and they that were ready went in with him to the marriage: and the door was shut. Afterward came also the other virgins, saying, Lord, Lord, open to us. But he answered and said, Verily I say unto you, I know you not. Watch therefore, for ye know neither the day nor the hour wherein the Son of man cometh.

We must do like this woman and the five wise virgins and shut the door on the naysayers who say we don't have a gift or a talent that will allow us to prosper. We must shut the door and go within and find out what hidden treasures lay within us. We must go within and develop our skills, clean up our houses (our consciousnesses), renew, and fine-tune it. We must borrow from our neighbors who have vessels of substance. Those are neighbors who have successful careers and wholesome family relationships, who demonstrate the fullness of life, exemplified in wealth, health, love, forgiveness, and faith in the impossible.

Like the woman in 2 Kings, we must pour into these vessels, into those around us and those with whom we do business, the gifts of the Spirit (*the oil of* patience, love, forgiveness, faith, long-suffering, charity, and wisdom). Like the woman in Luke 7:37 with the alabaster box of precious ointment, we must give all until it breaks open. It was not until after the woman in 2 Kings had exhausted all of the vessels that her blessing came.

Her blessing in the natural and the supernatural came while she was busy doing all she knew to do, all she was instructed to do; while she was *occupying* (as in Luke 19:13) the earth that God has given us did the blessing come. She used what she had. She operated on faith that since her house (her deceased husband, herself, and children) had served God, then the prophet must give her a blessing. She made a demand on the anointing, the prophet, the Christ consciousness within her, and told herself that she was entitled as a seed of Abraham to receive a blessing. She called it forth in faith, applied action to it, and it was so. From the exchange, believers can be assured that their seed will be blessed as well by going to the Father.

And lastly, the exchange will make it clear to the world that we are sons and daughters of God and it will be evident that the words we speak are the truth and will point the hearer to the Word of the Lord. The hearer should be left with a thirst to seek God and not the prophet. Like the exchange the woman at the well had with Jesus in John 4:14, it should leave the recipient with a desire to never thirst again.

If the following premise is true, this theory should not only be evident in my life, but also in the lives of all believers. If God's grace knows no boundaries, then this exchange should work not only in the inner cities of America but also in the destitute townships of South Africa or in the bleak ghettos of Russia. Believers should be able to answer the following four questions:

1. What is the blessing from the exchange of first fruits or a visitation with a prophet or minister in the natural and the supernatural?

2. Does the exchange deal with my fears of success; issues of poverty, sexism, racism, loneliness, and rejection; or general feelings of insecurity?

3. What favor is apparent for all to see?

4. Am I doing something of value, am I engaged in a profession of sorts, am I using what I have *to occupy until the blessing comes*?

I found I had no trouble answering these questions. The blessing I received from the exchange was a prophecy over my life that I would be a real estate broker and that people would be attracted to me. As I experienced success in sales, the fear inherent in undertaking a new career diminished. Success, however, does not come without a price tag. Sometimes it may cost the receiver a loss of friends or jealousy from coworkers, friends, or family members. During these times, I had to draw close to Christ and affirm that, like Paul, "if God be for us, who can be against us?" (Rom. 8:31). I had to accept that my true friends and loved ones would be happy for my success and would cheer me on. If they chose not to, I had to dig my spiritual roots down deep and know that God would resurrect "a ram in the bush" (Gen. 22:13) in the form of supportive and loving friends and family.

The exchange eliminated my fear of poverty and enabled me to pay off all of my credit cards and to make investments in real estate. Since becoming a regular giver of tithes and offerings, God has always given me much more in return. I can elaborate on several occasions where customers have called, with the deal already agreed on, in need of an agent to write up the transaction. I have experienced numerous deals that were not "sweat-of-my-brow" transactions, but definitely transactions demonstrating the favor of God at work in my life.

During the time that I was a single woman living in a world plagued with relaxed social and sexual mores, adultery, fornication, and HIV, my gift to sell real estate offered me a respite from these perils. My gift became like a best friend that gave me comfort. Sales can be an all-consuming profession, particularly so in this age of the Internet with the ability to sell globally. Instead of worrying about not having a date on Friday night, I enthusiastically and without regard to time would engross myself with making cold calls, showing houses, writing up contracts, or working on a business development plan.

As with overcoming my fear of success, God eventually supplied a "ram in the bush" again in the form of marriage to my husband, Tillmon H. Rosemon Jr., in 1992. I do want to emphasize that, like Abraham in Genesis 22:9–10, my husband came into my life as a result of sacrifice; I put God first and became almost indifferent about whether I married or not. I had to get to the point of acknowledging that "yes God, I would like a husband, but if You don't give me one, I will love You anyway." I am constantly amazed at the gifts God gives us.

Tillmon believed in me and, after our marriage, had the skills to open our real estate company. Wherein I was weak in what is required to successfully manage a company, Tillmon was strong and filled in the missing pieces. The amazing thing about our relationship was that I did not know that Tillmon had these qualities prior to our marriage.

I overcame my fears of rejection and general feelings of insecurity by embracing them and welcoming them into my life like an old friend. In sales, rejection and the resulting success that comes from overcoming one's fears and insecurities, are a necessary part of achieving one's goal. Having no present-day mentors that had gone down this path before me, I drew on biblical examples like David, Joseph, Job, Ruth, and Esther.

These individuals demonstrated how they dealt with and overcame falsehoods, jealousy, envy, abandonment, hatred, and revenge by applying the Word of God in their lives. I inferred that since there is nothing new under the sun, and that since God is no respecter of persons (Acts 10:34), then it stands to reason that if God blessed these individuals, He would definitely redeem me. I concluded that these historical lessons contained universal spiritual truths applicable to all who call themselves the seed of Abraham by faith.

The remarkable thing about overcoming these fears is that it leaves a roadmap, a sort of imprint on your spiritual synapses. What happens is that when these fears raise their ugly heads, you smile within yourself because you recognize FEAR as only an acronym for *False Evidence Appearing Real*. The smile or the laugh that comes to your face is because you know that this battle has already been defeated and that the battle is not yours, it's the Lord's. You accept that, in the spirit, the battle has already been won. It is simply a matter of time until you see the outward physical manifestation of the victory.

After reasoning that I could receive God's blessings, I had to ask myself how His favor was apparent in my life. There were numerous examples of favor subsequent to the prophecy over my life. When making cold calls, customers would agree to meet with me in person, which usually led to me listing their houses or engaging me as a buyer's agent.

When asked why they chose me, customers would say that they felt I displayed compassion, perception, insight, wisdom, understanding, or persuasive abilities, or that I had astute negotiating skills. Some were not able to delineate so clearly and would tell me it was my smile, the photo, the offer to provide honest service, or, surprisingly, that God told them to do so. These gifts enabled me to secure appointments and listings with potential sellers and buyers.

The prophecy over my life occurred on June 30, 1985, during a healing service held by the late Rev. Janet Sims, founding pastor of Jesus Christ Center of Truth in Atlanta, Georgia. She anointed me with oil and prophesized the following over me: "I waited patiently upon the Lord and He heard my cry." She saw me emotionally being healed and a relationship coming into my life—it would be crystal clear to me. She saw me teaching and people being more and more attracted to me. She saw me becoming a broker and having my own place. She told me to relax and get rest when I went home, to lie in the position of the cross. She said I knew what I wanted to do with my life and it was clear.

The prophecy was that simple and unexpected, particularly because I hadn't even studied for a broker's license.

The acknowledgment from fellow agents, senior agents, and brokers that there was something special about my ability to sell real estate became pivotal in my life along with this prophecy. I would involve myself in real estate related activities without regard to time or effort in order to bring them to fruition.

An additional endorsement came early in my career, just as I was establishing myself and had not become a million-dollar producer yet. A seller by the name of Carolyn Evans, a recent divorcée wanting to transition into a new career, asked me for advice on how to start a cleaning business. I shared with her techniques I had used as outlined in what I call my "Seven-Step Success Plan" (see page 60). Carolyn followed the plan and was quite successful. She wrote me a letter that I still treasure to this day. In it was an acknowledgment, a prophecy of sorts, that I would be successful in real estate because I cared about people as well as making money.

In summary, the exchange I had with the prophet, with the manifested Word, enabled me to answer all four of the questions that I posed earlier (see pages 7 and 8) and experience a blessing in the natural, as a successful real estate agent and broker, as well as in the spiritual realm. Likewise, you the reader must be able to receive from a prophet (perhaps your pastor or minister or the manifested Word) an exchange that leaves you with a clearly defined sense of purpose and vision for your life here on earth. The exchange you receive should also have eternal value and be a benefit to mankind.

It behooves the reader to make sure that your source of spiritual supply, your minister, and the spiritual teachings that you receive serve as a conduit that is able to draw out and facilitate an exchange. It is important that once you receive the exchange—the gift—that you keep God first and that you don't make the prophet, the minister, the job, or the gift your idol.

The following passage of Scripture has brought me a sense of hope and encouragement during times of despair and confusion:

> Sing, O barren woman, you who have never bore a child; burst into song, shout for joy, you who were never in labor; because more are the children of the desolate woman than of her who has a husband, Enlarge the place of your tent. . . . For you will spread out to the right and to the left; your descendants will dispossess nations and settle in their desolate cities . . . no weapon forged against you will prevail (Isa. 54:1–3, 17, NIV).

I pray this passage will give comfort to those who feel that their time has not come. To those who feel that they have not given birth to their dreams or aspirations: may you be encouraged to sing and rejoice before the battle that the victory is won, knowing that weeping may endure for a night, but joy will come in the morning! I am confident that if you faithfully make the exchange as outlined below in the Prayer of Agreement and complete the following exercises, in the fullness of time the desires of your heart will be manifested. This is God's promise to you and "God is not a man, that he should lie . . . hath he said, and shall he not do it? Or hath he spoken, and shall he not make it good?" (Num. 23:19).

Note: All Prayers of Agreement should be recited aloud.

Prayer of Agreement

I make the exchange now, Father. I agree to obey You and Your Word, and to love my neighbor as myself. I commit to tithe 10 percent of my gross earnings and to give an offering consistently without failure. I ask, Father, that You would reveal to me in the fullness of time the talent within me to prosper and to gain wealth. I commit to always acknowledge You as the source of my prosperity and to encourage others to prosper and succeed through Christ as well. I agree like the barren woman to sing now, to give thanks in a state of barrenness before the blessings are apparent in my life. All these blessings, or something better, let Your unlimited good will be done.

Exercise #1

Place pen and paper near your bed, then meditate and say out loud the following before retiring:

Heavenly Father, I ask that You would reveal to me how I can develop this seed within me to its full potential. Reveal to me, oh Father, what this gift is and how this gift can make me whole and prosperous, and able to impact the body of Christ in a positive, life-affirming way. Open my spiritual eyes, Father, that I may see the plan that You have ordained for me from the beginning of time to make me the head and not the tail. Make it plain how I may serve to spread Your Word and bring others to accept Christ that they may go forth and enjoy the abundant life.

Now expect to be awakened at night and be quick to write down dreams or thoughts that come to you. It is also a good idea to write down thoughts that come to you while listening to an inspirational message or song. Sometimes it is not so much what is *taught*, but what is *caught* during a time when you are mentally, spiritually, and physically in a state of preparedness. This is a form of *occupying until He comes*. Please note that this process may take weeks, months, or years. I know Americans don't like to wait, but God's command is to occupy until He comes. Like Abraham and Sarah we must be willing to wait, for the reward is definitely worth it.

Exercise #2

When you have determined what your gift is, you should be able to confidently and without hesitation or doubt in your mind answer the following questions:

1. What is the favor that is apparent for all to see, especially from strangers who acknowledge that I am gifted in a certain area?

2. What is the blessing from the exchange of first fruits or the prophecy spoken over my life?

3. The exchange enables me to deal with obstacles in my life including my fears of success, poverty, loneliness, rejection, or general feelings of insecurity as follows:

4. Is the exchange that I have received producing food and favor in the natural and supernatural? If so, how?

5. During times of scarcity in my life, is there substance in my house, i.e., physical substance, resources, spiritual strength, or creative ideas to prosper myself and to help others?

6. What is my vision that seems impossible or larger than life to perform?

7. Am I clueless as to how to accomplish it, but I feel a gnawing within me that I must do it, or at least try?

8. By faith I am doing the following to occupy until the blessing comes:

9. Have I trimmed my lamps like the five wise virgins and exhausted my vessels by pouring into those around me the oil of love, forgiveness, patience, faith, and wisdom?

10. I am borrowing the following from my neighbors who have vessels of substance:

11. Do onlookers see the Christ in me first and foremost, or do they see someone seeking the exchange or the prophet?

12. Is it clear to onlookers that I am the son or daughter of the Most High and do I leave them with a thirst to seek Jesus?

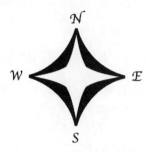

Chapter 2

Realization of Your Breakthrough

And God said, let the earth bring forth grass, the herb yielding seed, and the fruit tree yielding fruit after his kind, *whose seed is in itself,* upon the earth: and it was so (Gen. 1:11).

What's in you? What is your anointing? Over the years I found that many Christians struggle with not knowing what their particular anointings are. I thought about calling this chapter, "What is Your Anointing?" or "Finding Your Anointing." I chose not to because I felt too many readers would become confused and intimidated (as I had been) by the word "anointing." The term "anointing" for many, I felt, would be too spiritual. It seemed to conjure up special people like Jesus, Moses, Mahalia Jackson, or Billy Graham. The term "anointing" in relation to being "anointed to sell real estate," "anointed to play golf," or "anointed to clean houses" seemed a sacrilegious use of the word.

I now understand it as the special unique gift that God has placed within us. This gift has a physical as well as a spiritual component as explained in Genesis 1:11: "And God said, 'Let the earth bring forth grass, the herb yielding seed, and the fruit tree yielding fruit after his kind, whose seed is in itself, upon the earth:' and it was so." In the natural world, a female child at birth has all the eggs that she will need for life. Likewise in the spiritual realm, all your seeds are already in you. *Your seed—your ability to prosper, to reproduce, and multiply—is already in you.*

Although the female is the seed carrier in the natural, the male reproductive system is essential to the perpetuation of life. The female is dependent on the male for fertilization of her egg, even though it is she who carries the offspring through pregnancy and childbirth. Likewise in the spirit realm, we are dependent on Christ; He is our propitiator, He is the sacrificial lamb sent so that we can partake of an abundant life here on earth and life eternal in heaven.

It is crucial that as Christians we must understand that the seed is in us already. The seed in you is after your kind, i.e. the Christ. In 1 Corinthians 3:23, we are told, "and ye are Christ's and Christ is God's." In the Old Testament, Psalms 82:6–8, we are told ". . . ye are gods; and all of you are children of the Most High . . . for thou shalt inherit all nations." From the very beginning, in our spiritual DNA we already have in us what we need to sustain and overcome triumphantly the vicissitudes of life. Created within each of us is the challenging spirit that says, "I can do all things through Christ who strengtheneth me" (Phil. 4:13).

Put another way, this truth is revealed in John 1:16 wherein we are told, "of his fullness have all we received." I marvel that at the very beginning God provided all that we need. He tells us that we have everything that is of God already in us: His peace, love, patience, forgiveness, healing, prosperity, wisdom, kindness, and faith. All that God is we have—pressed down, shaken together, and running over (Luke 6:38). All we have to do as believers is claim our inheritance as a seed of Abraham, become grafted into the body of Christ, and be filled with the Holy Ghost. Then His fullness is ours. Said another way, we are told if we seek first the kingdom of God and His righteousness (right thinking, right acting, right believing), all things would be added (Matt. 6:33). All that we need, He provides. His fullness is then ours.

It is important to distinguish between someone who is gifted in an area and someone who is anointed in an area. Both qualities will attract onlookers and resemble each other. This was displayed in Exodus 7:11–12 when Pharaoh summoned his magicians to duplicate what Moses did with his rod. The difference as I see it, or the uncommon denominator, is that the anointing is able to destroy yokes (such as when Aaron's rod swallowed up and destroyed the magicians' rods). The anointing is able to do supernatural things, such as mobilize blacks and whites to overturn discrimination and desegregation laws through a Dr. Martin Luther King Jr., work healing through a Katherine Kuhlman, or work through a T. D. Jakes to empower homeless and jobless people to become property owners.

In a time of famine, there is always bread in the households of the anointed. They become lenders. Their anointing stands the test of time. Although they experience hardships and may be imprisoned like Joseph, in the end they become rulers over much and leave an inheritance for their children's children. Although they may have competitors that imitate them, their rod (their gift, their anointing) is able to devour their enemies, as Moses demonstrated with the magicians. They also feed the widows and the poor, and leave some behind for the gleaners. They become springs of water leading to eternal life (John 4:14).

According to Galatians 3:13–14, we are told that we are the seed of Abraham by faith in Christ Jesus. As heirs of Abraham, we are entitled to the promise of the receipt of the Comforter, which is the Holy Ghost and receipt of the gifts of the Spirit as sons and daughters of God (1 Cor. 12:7–13). This promise and these gifts enable us to achieve our goals, destroy yokes of bondage, live our dreams, and leave an inheritance to our children.

My realization of my anointing was slow in coming. Although I had been anointed by a minister to be a broker and to help people, I did not come to an acceptance of this anointing until more than twenty years after the prophecy had been spoken over me. Early in my real estate career, fellow agents and clients told me I had a special calling, a special ability to sell real estate. This meant little to me because my sales were flat. In 1986, my first year full-time in real estate, I only earned about eight thousand dollars. As time proceeded, the prophecy over my life faded into the memory of a Sunday service that was nice and boosted my ego, but meant little because the manifestation of this gift was not apparent to me.

Although my sales were negligible and infrequent, and nowhere near the status of a top producer, I was called on often by fellow agents to help them write sales transactions. I spoke recently to an agent, Liz Johnson, at a competing company. I had forgotten about working together on a transaction and had not remembered her. She told me that she has been holding on to a contract that I wrote nine years ago. Liz said that it was so well written that she still uses it as a guide in writing her contracts.

One incident I can recall occurred after I had made my first two sales, one to myself and another to a friend. With this "extensive" sales track record behind me, a senior agent at a prominent real estate firm approached me one day for help. Although this agent was one of the top producers at the firm, she had difficulty understanding and completing purchase and sale contracts. With the buyer in one room, she surreptitiously asked me to complete the contract in another room. This senior agent had found the purchaser a home but couldn't do the paperwork.

As time progressed, other agents would come to me and ask for my assistance. I still was nowhere near the status of a top producer, but the word was out there that I could and would help. As new agents came aboard my former office, which was a prominent national franchised firm in Atlanta with over fifty agents at that time, the broker would introduce me as someone new agents could come to for help. This was not an arrangement I had with the broker, nor was I compensated for my services, although it increased and contributed to my broker's bottom line.

I accepted this arrangement because I enjoyed helping agents to succeed. It was just in me to help. In retrospect, my willingness and enjoyment of this role are factors that were indicators of my anointing. As I matured, learned from others, received spiritual guidance and direction, continued to do what I enjoyed doing (occupying until He comes), and experienced success, year after year, I came to an acceptance of my anointing.

In 2001, the conclusive acceptance of my anointing came about from several events:

1. The company's growth in the number of agents requesting interviews for sales positions at Rainbow Realty. On average I interviewed one agent a week.

2. Agents drawn to me in large numbers would confirm that there was something special about me.

3. In January 2001, I began to share inspirational messages during sales meetings that God had revealed to me in what I called my "3 A.M. awakenings." From these inspirational messages, agents would take these thoughts and biblical truths, apply them to their lives and corresponding sales, and increased production would follow not only for them but also for me. The surprising thing about the increase in my sales production was that I was not actively soliciting business. The thought crossed my mind several times that if I missed sleep by getting up early in the morning, I would have less energy or my individual sales would slack off. Of course the thought occurred as well that my agents may not grasp or see any merit in what I was trying to convey to them. But the proof was in the pudding—my production level as well as my agents' accelerated.

These three events, along with the recollection of the anointing of oil and the prophecy that was spoken over me in 1985, made it crystal clear that this was my calling. Not only did I realize that I was gifted to sell real estate, but that I had an anointing to help others to sell and prosper their business. But more important was that I, as a real estate broker, would be used as a vehicle to bring other Christians to the Christ within themselves. As I had used the Word to prosper (to tithe myself out of poverty, to become a top producer, to open a prospering real estate firm, marry for the first time at the age of thirty-nine, give birth to our gifted son David at the age of forty-two), my accomplishments would help others to discover the Christ within them, find their anointing, and also the prosperity that God has promised for them as the seed of Abraham.

The following prayer and exercise are designed to help readers define and discover what their gifts and anointings are. I must emphasize that this process of self-discovery may take time and that it happens not according to our time, but according to God's time. Rest assured that God is always on time, that His ways are not our ways, and that His will is that we would prosper and be in good health (3 John 1:2).

Prayer of Agreement:

Father, I ask for Your guidance, Your direction in my life. I acknowledge that You have created me in Your image, after the seed of Abraham. In my mother's womb You formed my inward parts and placed Your seed within me. I pray now that You would reveal to me in due season the seed to prosper, the anointing on my life, the gifts that You have planted within me that I might have life and that more abundantly. Reveal to me, I pray, how I can develop this seed to its full potential. Reveal to me, oh Father, how this gift can impact the body of Christ and how it may serve to spread Your Word and bring others to accept the Christ that is within them. This or something better, Father, let Your unlimited good will be done.

Exercise

The following questions are designed to help you determine what your anointing is:

1. Do people, in particular strangers, confirm repeatedly that you have a special gift, calling, or ability to do something

that others don't do easily? For example, creatively cut shrubbery in a matter of minutes or design a greeting card that speaks comfort into someone's life? If yes, what are they saying?

2. Are you being uniquely you or are you copying someone else?

3. Would you perform your gift or talent, or exercise this ability without getting paid for it?

4. Do you do it in your sleep (i.e., think about it, dream about it)? Does it seem to be all consuming in your life? Are you enthusiastic about it?

5. Has an unsolicited prophecy been spoken over your life? If so, what was said?

6. Has God spoken to you? If so, what has He instructed you to do?

7. Has an unsolicited anointing been placed on you? Have you had a David experience as in 1 Samuel 16:1–13 where you are the ruddy one, the least desirable one, and you have been called out and anointed by a trusted minister or a prophet to do something that seems larger than life?

8. Do you know beyond a shadow of a doubt that your anointing is real, or is it a counterfeit?

9.   My gift is:

10.   My anointing is:

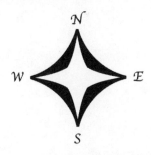

Chapter 3

Treasure Mapping for Success

Where there is no vision, the people perish (Prov. 29:18).

And the Lord answered me, and said Write the vision, make it plain upon tables, that he may run that readeth it. For the vision is yet for an appointed time but at the end it shall speak, and not lie: though it tarry, wait for it: because it will surely come, it will not tarry (Hab. 2:2–3).

What is your vision? What are you hungry for? In the early stages of my career as a full-time real estate agent, I was introduced to a concept of visualization. This was called treasure mapping in the book, *What Treasure Mapping Can Do For You*, by Mary Katherine MacDougall. The book essentially is an enactment of the verses from Proverbs 29:18 and Habakkuk 2:2–3 by combining the concept of speaking the Word, visualizing the Word pictorially, obeying God's Word, and waiting for the manifestation of the vision or goal. In her book, MacDougall shares numerous examples of individuals who have successfully treasure mapped for everything from jobs, cars, money, spouses, health, and businesses to prosperity in general. The example shown on the next page is the one I modified to treasure map for life membership in the DeKalb Board of Realtors Million Dollar Club in Atlanta, Georgia.

Reproduced by permission from What Treasure Mapping Can Do for You *by Mary Katherine MacDougall © 1968 by Unity School of Christianity.*

Please note that if you want to achieve your treasure map goal, open your own company, sit down at the banquet table of success, or achieve Million Dollar Club status (a recognition given each year by local board of realtors to recognize realtors who have sold over one million dollars in a calendar year), it will be in the presence of your enemies. Expect opposition, expect temptation, and expect resistance! Sometimes those enemies will be of your own household, i.e., your family, friends, love ones, etc.

Jesus himself was tempted in all manners known to man according to Hebrews 4:15. We must respond as Jesus did when we encounter obstacles to our treasure-map goals. Jesus dealt with temptation by identifying with what the Word said about Him, i.e., that He is the Head and not the tail. And as such, He has the power through God to put all manner of sickness, poverty, and evil under His feet.

Jesus knew the Word—He had studied it from childhood. When faced with opposition, He would call upon the Word. He knew within his innermost being that man shall not live by bread alone (carnal things—what we perceive with our senses as being true or news headlines, statistics, economic trends, etc.), but by every word that proceedeth out of the mouth of God (Matt. 4:4).

You, like Jesus, must spend time in the Word. If you don't know the Word, you don't know your inheritance, you don't know what spiritual armor you have, and you don't know what cities God has already placed in your hands (Deut. 6:1–11). Without knowledge of your birthright or your inheritance, you are clueless as to how to overcome the dark places in your life as you strive to achieve your goals.

Jesus took authority over obstacles in His life by speaking into the dark places of His life and acting according to the Word. Jesus took His lead from His Father, who when the earth was without form and void and darkness was upon the face of the waters said, "Let there be light: and there was light" (Gen. 1:3). Likewise, you like Jesus, must be able to say with authority, boldness, and discernment to the "Peters" (the dark places in you life), "Get thee behind me, Satan" (Mark 8:33) and "let there be light" (Gen. 1:3). You must know who you are and whose you are. You must know that as the seed of Abraham you can call on Jesus for wisdom, enlightenment, and courage to face the dark valleys in your life and accomplish your desires.

In the natural, God has given us lights in the firmament of heaven to divide the day from night. He said they were for signs and for seasons and for days and years (Gen. 1:15). In the spirit realm, the light God has given us is His spirit to lead, guide, and direct us. He gives us His Word as His rod to offer discernment, and His staff, the Holy Spirit as the Comforter. With this we can call forth light and rule over the dark places in our life. We use these spiritual tools to divide day from the night (to keep away the darkness from the bright, enjoyable times of our life). What is the darkness you want to rule over? Is it poverty, illness, fear, unhappy relationships, disease, or lack of confidence? What do yo want to place on your treasure map that you may gain the victory over?

The following two concepts are crucial and must be understood and applied on a daily basis in order to implement your desires on your treasure map:

1. **Know that if your vision is of value, there will be opposition.**
   When faced with opposition remember Psalm 23 and affirm aloud:

   The LORD is my shepherd. I shall not want. He maketh me to lie down in green pastures: he leadeth me beside the still waters. He restoreth my soul: he leadeth me in the paths of righteousness for his name's sake. Yea, though I walk through the valley of the shadow of death, I will fear no evil: for thou art with me; thy rod and thy staff they comfort me. *Thou preparest a table before me in the presence of mine enemies: thou anointest my head with oil*; my cup runneth over. Surely goodness and mercy shall follow me all the days of my life: and I will dwell in the house of the LORD forever.

   Know and expect opposition. It is in the presence of your enemies that you will achieve! God will anoint you in the presence of your enemies to do the task He requires of you. He will give you the oil of patience, endurance, love, and forgiveness so that you can stand and see God place your enemies under your feet (Ps. 110:1 NIV). By standing still, you will see the salvation of God. You will see God work on your behalf and see your enemies become your footstool.

2. **Know that there is an appointed time for your harvest.**
   When questioning the timing of God, read the following Scriptures and know that the same force that keeps the heavens in place and in order, continuously watches over you, His sheep:

   Is there any thing too hard for the Lord? At the time appointed I will return unto thee, according to the time of life, and Sarah shall have a son (Gen. 18:14).

   To every thing there is a season, and a time to every purpose under the heaven. A time to be born . . . (Eccl. 3:1–2).

   Thou shall arise, and have mercy on Zion: for the time to favour her; yea, the set time, is come (Ps. 102:13).

Even the stork in the sky knows her appointed seasons and the dove, the swift and the thrush observe the time (Jer. 8: NIV).

Therefore judge nothing before the appointed time; wait till the Lord comes. He will bring to light what is hidden in darkness (1 Cor. 4:5 NIV).

And God said, let there be lights in the firmament of heaven to divide the day from the night; and let them be for signs, and for seasons, and for days, and years (Gen.1:14).

The light reveals the appointed time, or the season. Know that your vision, when exposed to the light i.e., the Father, that it has an appointment to come forth into fruition. May it give you great comfort to know that not only does God watch over you, but He watches over His Word. He tells us in Jeremiah 1:12 ". . . I am watching to see my word is fulfilled" (NIV). In Isaiah 55:1, we are told, "So shall my word be that goeth out of my mouth, it shall not return unto me void, but it shall accomplish that which I please, and it shall prosper in the things where to I sent it." God has an obligation to fulfill His word. If you have a word, a promise from God, it must come true. In Mark 13:31 this truth is underscored as follows: "Heaven and earth shall pass away; but my word shall not pass away."

The treasure map I developed in the mid-1980s contained five main things I believed God would provide. They were: a commitment to keep God first in my life, a new car, a new house, a husband, and life membership in the Million Dollar Club. Suffice it to say, I received all of them in good measure.

Treasure Mapping Exercise

Now it is your turn to create your own personal treasure map. Psychological studies have shown that if a person commits an idea or a plan in writing there is a much greater likelihood that his or her vision will come to pass. You must impress upon your psyche that you mean business. You must harness your subconscious, conscious, and super-conscious mind and put them in subjection to your will, your vision. And, of course, this map must parallel God's will for your life.

For instance, if you are treasure mapping for a husband, you will affirm something like, "my divine mate comes forth now, we are in harmony with God and with one another." If your vision is for a car, your affirmation might read like this, "the perfect car now comes into my life. It is red, with a convertible top, and at the right terms and price." Be flexible and open as to how your blessings will come. Don't get specific as to how they will come into your life. The conduit may be a car auction, a gift from a friend, a purchase on time at a car dealership, or a loan from your credit union. At the center of your map should be a commitment to seek God and His righteousness first and His will for your life above all your requests on your treasure map.

If you need additional help, refer to Mary McDougall's book, *What Treasure Mapping Can Do For You,* and have fun. It is magical to see the invisible become visible! Once you have committed your vision to a treasure map, use the following Prayer of Agreement.

Prayer of Agreement:

(What follows is the prayer I used with my agents in a sales meeting after we had completed our treasure map as a cooperative group. You should modify the prayer to fit your vision and your personal treasure map or that of your company.)

Father, I now ask that if this vision is of You, that You would now bring forth these desires that we have laid out on our treasure maps. I ask that You would strengthen and empower us to do our parts to bring forth these desires. Reveal in the fullness of time how this will be accomplished.

Now you must say it and believe it. If you believe it, say with me now—call it forth now for yourself—what do you have to lose? You have everything to gain. Let us say it together with a loud voice. Let your enemies of doubt and disbelief scatter and run off. Let those enemies of fear flee from you. Fear is nothing but false evidence appearing as real. What is real is that we are sons and daughters of the Most High, we are the head and not the tail. If you believe, say with me now with a loud voice . . . *Listings, contracts, and closings cometh to me now.* (Substitute your desires from your personal treasure map in place of the real estate example I have given.) *Listings, contracts, and closings cometh to me now; listings, contracts, and closings cometh to me now; listings, contracts, and closings cometh to me now. Amen.*

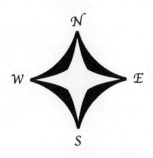

Chapter 4

Develop a Chaldean Approach to Life

For, lo, I raise up the Chaldeans, that bitter and hasty nation, which shall march through the breadth of the land, to possess the dwelling places that are not theirs . . .

Their horses also are swifter than the leopards, and are more fierce than the evening wolves: and their horsemen shall spread themselves; and their horsemen shall come from far; they shall fly as the eagle hasteth to eat . . . and they shall gather the captivity as the sand . . . And they shall scoff at the kings, and the princes shall be a scorn unto them: they shall deride every strong hold; for they shall heap dust and take it . . . Then shall his mind change, and he shall pass over, and offend, imputing this his power unto his god (Hab. 1:6–11).

I was inspired to write this chapter after hearing a sermon preached by the assistant pastor, D. E. Paulk, at the Cathedral of the Holy Spirit in Decatur, Georgia. In his sermon he described the Chaldeans, a heathen nation who fought against Judah. They were perceived as a formidable threat, possessing technology and weaponry that was advanced and far superior to anything known to man. Nothing was beyond their domination and all forces were subject to their authority. They even scoffed at kings and anyone in high authority. Like men at the Tower of Babel they had a mindset to dominate the world (Gen. 11:1–9). In a sense, they were gods unto themselves, worshipping idols, false gods, themselves, and their accomplishments. Pastor D. E. concluded by saying that we, as the body of Christ, should emulate the Chaldean attitude of world rule, but must not take on their godlessness.

I took his message a step further. We are told in the Old Testament that we were given the earth to possess it, to be fruitful and multiply. In the New Testament, Christ told us His part was finished. Christ left us the Comforter, which is the Holy Ghost, so that we would be empowered to put the government upon our shoulders, causing all forces and all nations to be subject to the name of Jesus. We must usher in the "every-knee-shall-bow, every-tongue-shall-confess-that-Jesus-Christ-is-Lord" (Phil. 2:10–11) by demonstrating the power of God in our lives, by overcoming evil with good.

We must show the world as a body of believers that we indeed are the head and not the tail. We show them by demonstrating mastery of our families and ourselves as in Daniel 1:1–20. Like the Israelites, we take care of our bodies so that they are stronger and last longer by eating the right foods. We are astute and have mastery of the "Chaldean" (i.e., the dominant) language, culture, and literature. Our women (seed carriers, idea carriers) must be fruitful, and not miscarry like the Egyptians in Exodus 1:19–20 and must not experience pain when they give birth. Whatever dream, vision, prophecy, or plan that we are carrying in our spirits is not aborted and comes to fruition. We don't experience the pain of giving birth to our ideas or our desires because the yoke, any bondage we find ourselves in, is destroyed because of the anointing on our lives.

We cast our cares on the Christ as Daniel did in the lion's den and we go free. We have intact, wholesome marriages and respectful, obedient, God-fearing children who graduate from the best schools. We are lenders and not borrowers. We make things happen, we are creative and talented leaders and inventors. We understand world systems, are astute politicians, and are infiltrators like Esther (Esther 4–7). We have our own businesses, and we are able to manage, invest, and multiply our talents as in the parable of the talents. If we are fired from or lose a job, we can open our own businesses and create new jobs for others.

We are capable of mastering everything from the White House to outer space. We train ourselves to possess everything that we tread upon. We are sons and daughters of the Most High. Since there is nothing too hard for God (Jer. 32:27), therefore there is nothing too hard for us through Jesus the Christ. We are not squeamish, passive Christians waiting for the by-and-by. We are visionaries. We are Martin Luther Kings, Mother Teresas, Rosa Parkses, Mahatma Gandhis. We are doers of the Word and not hearers that dress up and go to church Sunday after Sunday, bearing no fruit, but only the latest fashion outfit. Like Christ, we become the manifested Word.

We are Christ-empowered duplications of Bill Gates, Tiger Woods, Donald Trump, and Oprah Winfrey. I don't know who these successful individuals impute their power to prosper to. *But I do know that as believers, we should impute this power, this ability to gain wealth and to live long, prosperous lives to the one true living God, Jehovah Jireh, who sent His Son for the redemption of all mankind.* We acknowledge and accept our inheritance as the seed of Abraham. As the head goes, so goes the tail. We must be redeemers of mankind.

So how does one accomplish this as it relates to sales? How does one develop this Chaldean approach in one's everyday nine-to-five walk of life? In my arena of real estate sales, I started with a business plan and a mission statement under a Christian covering and anointing. Although my mission statement was corporate in nature, it could easily be modified to meet the individual needs by placing the subject in the first person.

Any successful entrepreneur knows the importance of having a written business plan along with a written mission statement. The combination of these two instruments under a Christian covering and anointing will give you a sense of direction—a road map—and should result in a written plan of action that will guide you to the fulfillment of your dream(s).

My plan of action evolved from the premise that man is composed of mind, body, and spirit. The training approach I used was designed to impact all three levels. We nourish the spirit through prayer, song, and sharing of inspirational messages. Two songs were sung regularly and were adopted as company theme songs. The first was, "I'm blessed, I'm blessed, I'm blessed" and the second was entitled, "Happy am I, I'm rich, I'm happy" (see appendix).

I addressed the mind by reminding agents who we are in Christ. At the opening of sales meetings, we affirmed aloud our mission statement, which read as follows:

"Our covenant is to establish a vehicle for real estate agents to become life members of the DeKalb Board of Realtors Million Dollar Club by empowering their customers, clients, and themselves to achieve home ownership, retirement planning, and entrepreneurial pursuits. Our commitment is to provide honest and superior real estate and ancillary services in the greater metropolitan Atlanta area and beyond."

I also used a modified version of an affirmation from the book *Telepsychics: The Magic Power of Perfect Living* to establish in our subconscious mind who we are in truth. I developed the following meditation that we professed together at the beginning of sales meetings:

Today is God's day. I choose happiness, success, prosperity, health, and peace of mind. I am divinely guided all day long, and whatever I do will prosper. Whenever my attention wanders away from my thoughts of success, peace, prosperity, health, or my good, I will immediately bring back my thoughts to the contemplation of God and His love, knowing that He careth for me. I am a spiritual magnet, attracting to myself customers and clients who want what I have to offer. I give better service every day. I am an outstanding success in all my undertakings. I bless and prosper all those who come into my office and also into my life. All these thoughts are now sinking into my subconscious mind, and they come forth as abundance, security, health, and peace of mind. It is wonderful!

In addition, we committed as a group to follow my "Seven-Step Success Plan" that I used to overcome an income of eight thousand dollars my first year in sales in 1986. I believe that if this plan is faithfully followed, anyone can come out of debt and achieve a six figure income. It took me personally from a lifestyle of literally living on high-interest credit cards to pay my mortgage, car note, tithe, offering, and other obligations to a lifestyle where I have one credit card as financial counselors often advise for emergencies or to use because of the benefits associated with a credit transaction.

Up until this point, the average person is probably saying, "I can do this, I can develop a mission statement, a business plan, sing songs, and repeat affirmations." We have lofty thoughts about what we want to be when we grow up and we sing songs to affirm our supposed belief system. That's basically what we do Sunday after Sunday. We sing songs and hear a good message that inspires us, but when we get home, we may have difficulty taking authority over the body, the flesh part of this equation. Few are willing to master the flesh, to die to the flesh, so that we might live and experience the good life. Remember, God takes the simple things to confound the wise (1 Cor. 1:27).

If we look at nature, there are irrefutable laws, such as the law of gravity. Something that goes up must come down because the law of gravity controls it. Likewise, in the plant world, if an acorn dies and falls into the ground, it will produce an oak tree. That's the law of nature, and it is irrefutable. Any scientist will agree to this and any kindergartner who has tried this experiment will tell you the same thing.

In the spirit realm, there are also spiritual laws contained and hidden in the Bible that are just as irrefutable. One of them, which we all know by heart, is that you reap what you sow. If you want more love, peace, and prosperity in your life, do the things that will promote and attract these qualities in your life.

What supersedes these physical and spiritual laws, however, are supernatural laws. These are the ones that confound the wise, the unexplainable ones that allow you to walk on water, come out of a fiery furnace unscathed without the smell of smoke on you, and die to the flesh yet live and have years restored to you.

There is something unexplainable that happens when we die to the flesh. We can lose weight, run marathons, endure pain, escape from slavery, or come out of prison. Like a consummate aerialist, we are able to let go of one swing, risking death and destruction, and by faith catch hold of another swing pushed to us by a seen or unseen partner at exactly the right time and speed to catch it.

This is what "occupying until He comes" is all about. It is giving oneself completely to your calling. You must become a workaholic (but not remain one) at some points in order to break through to certain stages of growth for your calling. There are probably some readers that are thinking right now that, "it doesn't take all that."

Well, yes, it does and no, it doesn't. You see, it took Thomas Edison, Bill Gates, Michael Jackson, Tiger Woods, Michael Jordan, T. D. Jakes, and Joyce Meyer "all that." But they were doing what they love. And when you are doing what you love, it's like a child at play who has no regard for time. Mature Christians, however, know that the "no, it doesn't" part of the equation is that when you are in covenant with God, He will give you supernatural gifts as he did with Katherine Kuhlman, Benny Hinn, T. D. Jakes, and Dr. Martin Luther King Jr. that will lighten your load. The caveat, which many of us forget, is that we must be in covenant with God and at His divine timing, all yokes of bondage are removed. It is then that you will prosper in ways you never dreamed of. This is when you receive, "the houses and cities that you haven't built" as mentioned in Deuteronomy 6:1–11.

But remember the supernatural blessings only come when you are sold out and occupying until He comes. There's a paradox that kicks in: it's when you are not necessarily looking for the blessing that the blessing finds you. The anointing that God gives is analogous to a story found in John 20:1–16 where Peter and John were both running to the tomb and John outran Peter. Just because you get to the tomb first like John (or get to the modern-day Church first) does not guarantee that you will be blessed! What matters is that you become like Peter and go into the tomb but you still must take it a step further and be like Mary. Peter and John believed that Jesus had risen, but Mary chose to stay and occupy the tomb. And by doing so, she found Jesus. It is while you are occupying that the blessings of God outrun and overtake you. It is something that can't be explained in the natural because it is not of the natural, it is of the spirit.

The exercise at the end of this chapter is the Chaldean approach I took to accomplishing my goals in terms of dying to self. It is the occupying-until-He-comes part; the meat-and-potatoes part. This is what I describe as building an ark for one hundred years like Noah when you don't see even the first cloud in the sky. This is the doing part, the part where most people lose faith and say, "I'm too old, too young, not smart enough, I'm the wrong color or gender, or maybe God didn't mean what He said." This is the Sarah part where many say, "I guess I'll have to help God out, I can't give birth to this dream, so I'll let my bondwoman go in and fulfill a role that only can be fulfilled by that individual who is willing to die to self and the world's belief systems."

Earlier in chapter 2, I established that in Genesis, we are told that the seed is in itself. Each individual is earmarked with a task that is unique to him or her. Only that individual can give birth to a plan that has been preordained by God. Although we are made in the image and likeness of God, He has given us free will and we are not robots. God loves us too much to force us to serve Him. We can only fulfill our spiritual DNA, our destiny, our calling, and our anointing by making a conscious choice to do so. We must choose to occupy, to fight the good fight of faith.

We must occupy until He comes not only in the natural, but more important, we must occupy in the spirit realm. Billy Graham has been telling this nation to occupy for many years, but his "won't you come to Christ" is seen by many as too hokey. Bishop Earl Paulk, of the Cathedral of the Holy Spirit in Decatur, Georgia, has been preaching for years to occupy by coming into agreement, that regardless of our race, we are of one blood through the Abrahamic covenant. But this prophet continues to endure criticism by both some whites and blacks that still want separation of the races.

Bishop T. D. Jakes has told us to occupy since the mid-1990s with his declarations of "get ready, get ready!" Indicative that we are in the last days prior to the return of Christ, and in accordance with prophetic Scriptures, he told the women of the world that they "are loosed" from any type of bondage or affliction. But Bishop Jakes' message is seen by some as too emotional, too loud, too radical, or too female oriented.

And now another prophet comes on the scene; by the name of Juanita Bynum. (Juanita in Spanish is translated literally as the female version of little John.) Like a fiery John the Baptist, she preaches that we are to occupy by crucifying the flesh, trimming our lamps, and clinging to the altar. But many ears are closed to her message. It is seen by some as too much of a sacrifice for Christians who want to be Sunday Christians for one hour, but not Christian warriors. She, too, is seen as too loud, too demonstrative, too wild, and—of all things—she is a woman.

When will we as the body of Christ, as a Christian nation, get ready and occupy until He comes? When will we commit our lives to Christ and demonstrate to the nations of the world that regardless of our race, gender, or background that we are one blood redeemed at the cross? When will we show the world that we are indeed the head and not the tail, prepared to die to the flesh so that others might come to know Christ? When will we take on a Chaldean spirit that imputes our power to God?

CHALDEAN PLAN OF ACTION/SALES APPROACH

1. Owe No Man Any Thing, But To Love Him (Rom. 13:8)

Render unto Caesar the things that are Caesar's, and to God the things that are God's. In other words, pay your taxes and bills on time and stay in covenant with God by being obedient to His Word. Follow the Golden Rule, give your tithes and offerings, and learn to die to self and let the gifts of the Spirit work in and through you. But most important, follow the advice found in 1 Corinthians 12–13, to follow the more excellent way of love in all your thoughts and actions.

In order for your Chaldean business plan to be effective, at some point you will probably need credit to finance your vision. It is a well-known tenet in the business world that a prudent entrepreneur should use other people's money to finance one's dreams. If your credit history says you are a bad credit risk, you are that much farther from accomplishing your goals. Start today by ripping up your credit cards (save one for emergencies), delaying gratification, and buying only what you can afford using cash. Use the 80–10–10 rule. Tithe 10 percent to your church plus an offering, put 10 percent in savings (set aside for invest-ment opportunities), and live off of the remaining 80 percent.

2. Develop a Mission Statement, Business Plan, and Plan of Action

Before taking this next step, be sure that you have completed the exercises at the end of chapters 1 through 3. It is important that you not rush this process. The steps involved in identifying your gift and your anointing may take months or years. The receipt of an unso-licited prophecy, as explained in chapter 3 is just that: unsolicited. It is like the wind, you can't see it coming or going, you simply feel it or see its effects. Like the wind, it may blow or it may not. A prophecy over one's life does not have to be a prerequisite to discov-ering your gift or anointing. Like Samuel in 1 Samuel 3:1–10, God may simply tell you himself.

Once you know and have verified what they are, however, you can then define and put in writing your mission statement, business plan, and plan of action. At this point, if you experience difficulty putting them in operational terms, I would suggest that you take a business course at a local community college or institution that offers adult education classes with a focus on career development and business planning.

3. Prospect, Prospect, Prospect

Everyone is a potential customer or client. Start with everyone you know. Develop a written list of these individuals. They will become your sphere of influence. The high-tech, high-touch approach is best. Former President Clinton, I'm told, kept his contacts on a large index card roller. With time and the accumulation of names, this becomes cumbersome and ineffective. Like Clinton, I started initially with a small index card box in which I manually entered names and used date markers to follow up on prospects.

A prudent entrepreneur must use the available technology at hand, as the Chaldeans did in their time. If you want to see impressive results, you must use the technology that is engineered for that purpose. As my sales grew, I invested in real estate–specific contact and sales management software systems. This software package is like having a highly efficient administrative assistant that never forgets anything.

Some of the features of these products are a flyer and postcard library, a letter library of over seven hundred letters, a daily planner and organizer, an address book with a notes manager, buyer and seller action plans, buyer presentation and comparative market analysis features, referral tracker, an income and expense tracker, and a cold-calling telemarketing system that allows you to dial out directly from your computer to your prospect. It is a system that you can synchronize with other computers and allows you to add on other highly effective software products. This is just one example of the technology available to aid us in our goals.

In addition, a salesperson's basic arsenal of equipment should also include an Internet-based personal computer, a cell phone, a pager, and a digital camera. As technology changes, the entrepreneur must assess the effectiveness of new products in relation to what you presently have. That may involve adding on or taking away from what you already have. Remember, though, that it makes no sense to spend money on a product and not use it. I have seen too many salespersons go to a seminar, buy the product, and then not read the manual and struggle until a level of competency is reached.

It is analogous to going to church and hearing a message on becoming the head, but when you go home you don't practice the principles. You won't read your Bible and digest it. You won't put God to the test by doing your part and believing by faith that God will do His part. You won't die to self, to the flesh. You won't develop an attitude of divine indifference that says, "God, if you don't give me my desires, I'll love you anyway."

4. Marketing and Self Promotion

How do you let the world know that you have something of value to give to them? First of all, let me say that one must be prudent and wise when it comes to spending money for advertising. There are a lot of advertising vehicles that will pursue you with promises to increase your sales. It is important to be vigilant and keep track of where your sales and leads come from. You must know instinctively what causes your phone to ring and when to embark on a new advertising idea.

I will detail below what worked for me, but readers should bear in mind that they must assess not only for their business, but for their personality, what is most effective for them. Case in point: If you do not like working with buyers, you do not want to run ads, such as a home-buyer seminar, that will attract them. It is also important to learn to say "no, thank you" without comprising your business or religious convictions. If the shoe doesn't fit, don't put it on. As you experience more and more success, advertising opportunities will be drawn to you. Also, it may help you to stay on track by having someone with a similar belief system or training to field your calls.

The most cost-effective return on the dollar for me, prioritized by cost from the least to the most, has been word-of-mouth, cold calling, yard signs, property flyers, multiple-listing services, relocation services, professional organizations, mass mail outs, local trade magazines, Internet web sites, and the yellow pages (online and hard copy).

Two resources that I have not used are billboards or the purchase of a franchise. The results of my tracking efforts and research showed that these two methods did not offer a good return on the dollar. In regard to buying a franchise, my experience in working for over ten years with the two largest real-estate franchise companies in North America was that I could do more without them. My tracking showed that customers were coming to me because of my direct marketing efforts and it was extremely important to me to establish my own brand identity and niche marketing. My satisfaction came from doing it my way with God's help. I felt that the general public was more influenced by the qualities I possessed of honesty, and experience, and the industry designations and accomplishments that I had achieved.

5. Physical Exercise, Recreation, and Meditation

Suffice it to say that exercise and recreation are pivotal to your success in your career. Numerous books have been written about the importance of diet and exercise and the need for re-creation, i.e., getting away, being a child, resting from your labor, and just enjoying life. It is at these times of rest that you are free to recreate or, as the dictionary defines, "to create anew." Many of my best ideas have come during a period of rest. It has served to rejuvenate me with new ideas and vitality. Regular exercise and recreational activities must be built into your schedule and treated just like an appointment with a very important client.

Most people understand the definition of recreation, that it usually involves doing something and not necessarily sitting in a chair in front of the television. Recreation and rest, however, can be that for some individuals, particularly if their employment or daily routine is such that they never get to watch television or sit down and read a good book. Recreation can also be sedentary if it exercises and challenges your mind as in completing a large puzzle or playing a game of chess.

The crucial thing is that the individual should routinely engage in some form of regular bodily, physical exercise and engage in a recreational activity that is apart from one's daily work schedule. It should either challenge you mentally or raise your heart rate to an optimal level based on your age and health status. This recreational activity should allow you to have fun, let your hair down, become a child again, and lose yourself.

Studies have shown that those who engage in meditation typically live longer and healthier lives. At the beginning of sales meetings, we have a time of meditation. They vary and at times I have a standard one, or one that reflects the current status quo. I also use singing as a form of relaxation.

I strongly urge the reader to have a time set aside each day to meditate, read the Bible, and sing unto the Lord. Nehemiah 8:10 tells us that "the joy of the Lord is your strength." This being the case, then we must, like David, encourage ourselves and stir up the gifts of the Lord in us in times of adversity (1 Sam. 30:6; 2 Tim. 1:6).

Chaldean Prayer of Agreement:

Holy Spirit, we ask that You would grace us with Your presence. We usher You in with joy, with thanksgiving, with peace within our hearts and minds for all that You have already done. Let us, according to Your Word, dwell in peace with all brethren. Create in us a clean heart and renew a right spirit within us. Father, in Your name and in Your authority, I cast out every negative, contrary spirit that is not like You, I curse it at its root and I command it in Your name to be dissolved into nothingness, not by might nor by our power, but by Your Spirit. By Your Spirit that is able to melt away bitterness, envy, jealousy, and unkindness.

Having cleansed ourselves, I ask You, Father, to release the fruits of Your Spirit, which are peace, love, joy, patience, wisdom, understanding, faith, kindness, and the ability to prosper. Father, in Your name I command the anointing to prosper that You have placed on me, to be placed also on these agents. Make them winners, make them all life members of the Million Dollar Club [substitute your desire here]. *Equip them with health, sharpness of mind, discernment, diplomacy of spirit, and kindness of heart; with a knowingness in the spirit that as they give, not just in fulfilling the law of their tithes and offerings, but as they give of their hearts, that Your promise is to give good measure, pressed down, shaken together, and running over.*

Father make us the head and not the tail, by doing what the head does, by following Your Word. Father, in all our getting, let us get understanding, make us to know that the greatest gift is not money or fame but it is love, for only what we do for Christ will last.

Father, we accept that You have heard our prayer, we accept that it is already done. So we stand on Your Word and we give thanks. Weeping may endure for a night, but joy cometh in the morning. Father, we accept that we will shed some tears in bringing forth this harvest, but we focus on Your Word that says it is already done, so we stand and we rejoice. We don't focus on any problems at hand, but we hold true to Your promise of victory and we rejoice knowing that the battle is not ours but the Lord's. So in spite of our circumstances, we rejoice and know that it is already done in the spirit and that it is only a matter of time before it is manifested in the natural.

And when the manifestation comes, we make this commitment now, Father, to be like the leper that returned and gave thanks. We make a commitment now, Father, to acknowledge You as the source, we impute this power to You, as the One that gave us this ability to prosper, as the One that gave us favor with men, as the One that put our names on clients' mouths to call us for their services, and to refer other customers to us. Great is your faithfulness, Father, to us; may we be found faithful doers of Your Word and not hearers only.

Chaldean Arsenal Checklist

1. Are you in covenant by giving your tithes
   and offering, whether on vacation or not?   ____ yes ____ no
2. Are you current with your taxes and have
   you given Caesar his due?   ____ yes ____ no
3. Have you taken the first step by committing
   in writing your mission statement, business plan,
   and plan of action?   ____ yes ____ no
4. Have you developed a list of your sphere of
   influence?   ____ yes ____ no
5. Do you speak the Chaldean language fluently? ____ yes ____ no
6. Are you computer literate?   ____ yes ____ no
7. Have you entered your prospects into a
   contact-management system?   ____ yes ____ no
8. Does your system contain features such as a
   letter and postcard library, anniversary
   features for birthdays and job promotions, and
   an income and expense tracker?   ____ yes ____ no
9. Are you cold calling on a regular basis via the
   telephone, mail, E-mail, or in person?   ____ yes ____ no
10. Are you regularly attending seminars and
    educational conferences so that you can stay
    abreast of the latest changes and technological
    advances in your industry?   ____ yes ____ no

11. Are you up to par with any designations or
certifications that reflect the industry standard of
competency or excellence for your
profession or trade? ____ yes ____ no
12. Are you partnering with significant others? ____ yes ____ no
13. Are you regularly advertising your product
and spending your money in the most
cost-effective ways? Are you getting the best
return on your dollar through your
advertising efforts based on a tried and tested
tracking system? ____ yes ____ no
14. Do you offer discounts or have sale items
(if appropriate)? ____ yes ____ no
15. Is franchising a viable way to achieve your
goals? ____ yes ____ no
16. Do you attribute your ability to gain wealth
to God? ____ yes ____ no
17. Are you taking dominion over secular
systems and spiritual debacles? ____ yes ____ no
18. Are you becoming the head and not the tail? ____ yes ____ no
19. Have you been redeemed at the cross? ____ yes ____ no
20. Are you able to exchange your gift,
your trade, without regard to barriers of
race, gender, class, sexual orientation,
or background? ____ yes ____ no
21. Are you appropriating enough time in your
schedule for rest, meditation, mental and
physical exercise, and recreation? ____ yes ____ no
22. Do you have a daily time of fellowship with
God, through reading His Word, meditating,
and singing praises unto God? ____ yes ____ no
23. Have you left something behind for the
gleaners? ____ yes ____ no

Chapter 5

Partnering with Others

And five of you shall chase an hundred, and a hundred of you shall put ten thousand to flight; and your enemies shall fall before you by the sword (Lev. 26:8).

Partnering is analogous to weaving a spider's web. What is central to each web is that Christ is the main artery and the heart that distributes blood through every vein of the web, pumping energy and faith and life into every thread of the web. Jill Bailey, in her book, *How Spiders Make Their Webs,* unfolds a mystery of the natural world of the spider that shows how spiders use silk to build their homes, hunt and trap prey, protect their eggs, and signal to potential mates. The spider has an ecosystem in the natural that is worth paralleling in the spiritual realm.

Ms. Bailey, in her book, explains that spiders produce silk to make their webs. This silk is really a protein called fibroin. Spider silk is extremely strong—a length of silk would have to be over fifty miles long before it would break under its own weight. This means that when some unfortunate creature blunders into a spider's web, the web stretches rather than breaks. The silk is produced as a liquid by special glands inside the spider's abdomen. These glands are linked to tube-like organs called spinnerets. The angle of the spinnerets is controlled by muscles and can be varied at will. Once the liquid silk is exposed to the air, it hardens into a thread.

One of the most intricately constructed spider webs (found in most parts of the world) is the orb web, in which a spiral of silk is laid around a series of silk spokes that spread out from a central point. Bailey says, interestingly enough, to start an orb web, like the aerialist mentioned in chapter 4, the spider must first make a bridge line between two high points. It then lets loose a silk thread onto the breeze and hopes it catches on a suitable object, or it may travel with the thread to the second anchor point. The spider now travels back along the first line, spinning a stronger thread, which it leaves dangling below it.

The spider then returns to the middle of the line, grasps this thread, and drops to the ground or to a suitable twig or leaf. This forms the third anchor point and resembles a triangle. In the natural world we have a basic strong geometric pattern (the same one the Egyptians used to build the pyramids), but in the spiritual realm we have a reflection of an anchor composed of the Father, Son, and the Holy Ghost as being the skeletal model we should follow in partnering.

According to Ms. Bailey, the spider next makes a series of extra framework threads around the outside and lays down the radial threads, working from the center outward, and anchoring them to the basic framework. So far, all the silk used up to this point has been dry, not sticky. The spider then makes a tight spiral in the center of the web to anchor the radials and reinforce them. Further out, the spider makes a widely spaced temporary spiral, working around from the inner part of the web. The gap between the outer spiral and the inner spiral will allow the spider to cross from one side of the web to the other later.

Once we build our vision upon the rock, which is Jesus Christ, and have the Father and the Holy Ghost as part of our foundational belief system, we can begin our series of extra framework threads and lay down our radial threads like the spider. Our dry silk, our protein that we use, must be the Word of God. Like the spider, we must remember to always work from the center outward and anchor them to our belief system. This does not mean we can't partner with nonbelievers, but it does mean that believers and nonbelievers alike must be trustworthy, ethical, and adhere to our vision.

Returning to the example above, our substitution for the tight spiral in the center of our web must be the application of the Word of God. We must speak the Word, believe in the Word, and take action like the aerialist and physically launch out and make our dreams happen. This will allow us to cross from one side of the web to the other, or from one challenge to the next.

Ms. Bailey reports that the final stage of building the spider web involves making the sticky catching spiral. Glue-covered threads of silk produced by a different set of the spider's silk glands are carefully attached to the radials to form a tight spiral. The spider works from the outside toward the hub, *eating the silk* from the temporary spiral as it goes. As the spider attaches the threads of the sticky spiral, it plucks them sharply with a claw. This causes the glue to break up into separate droplets.

In the spirit realm, our sticky catching spiral metaphorically comes from our abdomen as well. Jesus said that out of our belly would "flow rivers of living waters" (John 7:38). We must, like the spider, eat our silk. To gain whatever is precious to us, we may have to endure rejection, criticism, false accusations, and hatred, and die to self. We build our sticky catching spiral by applying love, joy, peace, and long-suffering, i.e., the fruits of the Spirit (Gal. 5:22).

Ms. Bailey goes on to describe that with this web now complete, the spider sits in the center, the reinforced platform, and waits for prey to approach and get caught in this sticky web. One of the fascinating things about most spiders is that although they have eight legs and eight eyes, they do not rely on vision to detect prey. Instead, they use the vibrations of the web caused by the struggling creature. The spider rests on the center platform in the web, or in a retreat close by, resting a leg on one of the silk threads. The slightest vibration of the web sends a signal along this thread. By testing the tension of the various threads, the spider can tell exactly where the prey is trapped. Small prey will be bitten immediately, *but larger ones will be bound with silk first* to prevent them from escaping.

We as the body of Christ must begin to work more in the spirit realm and stop relying solely on what we see. We must trust the vibrations of the Spirit. When our web—our business, marriage, children, or finances—cause us irritation, pain, and distress, we must recognize that what the Bible says is true: "Ye thought evil against me; but God meant it unto good, . . . to save much people alive" (Gen. 50:20). We must immediately get rid of pettiness and small thinking. This may include separating ourselves from individuals, friends, or family members who don't understand our vision and would hinder our destiny. Like the spider, we must save the bulk of our silk, our love, and build ourselves up spiritually in order to take on the demons in our life with love, patience, wisdom, and forgiveness. We must learn how to love the hell out of our enemies so that we can occupy and take dominion over world systems as God commanded us to do in Genesis 1:26–28.

People will come and go in your life and will constitute different parts of your web. Each thread is important and has a part to play. At times your web may give way and tear, but with Christ it can be repaired and restored to a thicker and stronger web. Patience is vital in building this web. Remember Rome wasn't built in a day.

We start the building of our web by agreeing, as detailed in chapter 1, that God has called us forth as the seed of Abraham. As such, we agree that He has given us the power to gain wealth. Chapter 2 tells us that His seed is in us already and has been established and preordained prior to being in our mother's womb. We agreed to occupy until it is crystal clear what our anointing is. In chapter 3, we made a commitment to write down the vision and orally call it forth daily and take steps to work towards its fulfillment. In chapter 4, we made a commitment to take a Chaldean approach to life and impute our gains, our success, to Christ. And now in this chapter, our task is to establish and weave together the necessary components to complete our own unique web, with our relationship with Christ as the foundation.

Before I do that, however, I want to digress for a moment and use the life of Dr. Martin Luther King Jr. as an illustration to demonstrate how he used this principle of partnering to overcome his enemies and to come out on top as the head. I will also walk the reader through Dr. King's life and show how it is a working illustration of the principles laid out in the ten chapters of this book.

Biographies on Dr. King's life have substantiated that Dr. King fell into a position of leadership as he preached and went from city to city. He realized early in his life that he had a call to preach (chap. 1). His breakthrough (chap. 2), however, came as he went from city to city and he came to himself; that is an understanding and accept- ance of his anointing to set at liberty those who were bruised. (In Luke 17:14, we are told that healing took place *as they went.*) Dr. King verbalized, preached, and played out his dream—his treasure map, if you will—that all men and women, black or white, Jew or Gentile, would be equal and judged by their character and not their outward appearance (chap. 3). He received his doctorate degree from Boston University and was able to relate to street people or presidents. Dr. King imputed his Chaldean gains to God (chap. 4). Dr. King part- nered with others and sold them on the use of the silk of love, forgiveness, wisdom, and patience to bind large enemies (chap. 5). Dr. King submitted himself to this bruising process (chap. 6) and was able to destroy the yokes of bondage in his life and for people all over the world. He did it by dying to self! He endured racial epithets, stones thrown at him, dog attacks, being placed in jail, and ultimately, being slain by an assassin's bullet.

Dr. King encouraged his partners to use the weapon of forgive- ness (chap. 7). Not only did he preach love your enemies, but he demonstrated love and forgiveness in his daily walk. He stood up to his enemies and demonstrated and became a role model of the more excellent way. That is, he displayed the fruit of the Spirit, which is love (chap. 8). Dr. King made the song, "We Shall Overcome," famous. By using the weapon of praise (chap. 9), he was able to overcome and make his enemies his footstool. We now reap the benefits worldwide and live in a much freer society; we are fast approaching the realiza- tion of his dream (chap. 10), not only in the natural, but more important, in the spirit realm where there is no distinction between black and white, male and female, Jew and Gentile as prophesied by Joel and emphasized in Acts 2:16–18.

Returning to our discussion of partnering, I want to expound on how we can establish and build our spider web so that we build our businesses and fulfill our destinies through the use of technology and human alliances. Partnering, or networking, is an important component of a good business plan. In most markets, it is necessary to form a partnership of some type in order to make a base income of six figures. I define partnering as being in unity with an individual or group or the use of technological aids that can assist an individual in obtaining a high, productive sales volume that alone they would be unable to achieve.

Partnership is an element that is difficult to develop, foster, and maintain. Sales, however, is basically a solitary career. Although an agent may employ supportive staff, ultimately the sales transaction involves a customer or client wanting to use an individual as a conduit to make an exchange for something of value.

In the 1990s we saw the emergence of the "mega agent" in real estate. This term is defined as one agent who has a team composed of a combination of licensed and unlicensed assistants. These assistants work under the mega agent in a supportive role of prospecting, listing, showing properties, advertising, and general clerical duties. All of this is done in the name of the mega agent. Although these individuals may be in the front office or behind the scenes, the one common thread is that everything they do is in the name of the mega agent. Like the spider's web, these are your radial threads that you employ so that you can apply the "sticky catching spiral" and do what you do best: negotiating, writing up contracts, and closing deals with prospects.

The question arises as to how to form these partnerships. The technological alliance is fairly simple. It involves some homework and may constitute attending workshops, continuing education classes, trade shows, and basically assessing what technological aids best suit you or your company's needs. Cost of the software is not necessarily indicative of value, usefulness, or effectiveness. Be careful not to get caught up in buying expensive software or products that move you away from your primary goal of finalizing a transaction with a customer. You must remain in control and at the helm of your ship.

The human and spiritual elements of your web are by far the most difficult to master, in part, because they can transcend so many different boundaries—marital, racial, religious, ethnic, gender, economic, political, class, ideological, and social. What is crucial and foremost is that Christ is at the center of your web and that He is your ultimate partner. This union never changes. Like a prism that reflects light from all angles, one should always be able to see the Christ in you.

Of course not all alliances serve in a supportive capacity but can oppose or be detrimental to your attempts to bring your vision into fruition. For example, your perception may be that your marital partner does not share your vision. You may perceive that the economy, the current political climate, or religious, familial, or social traditions don't line up with your dreams. It may be that no one of your race, gender, family, or social class has attempted to do what you are trying to accomplish.

When you perceive that there are opposing forces to your dream you must go back to chapters 1 and 2 in this book and ask yourself these questions: *Do I believe that God has put this desire in my heart? Do I believe that I have an anointing to bring these desires into fruition?* If so, then God promises to remove any yokes that come against the manifestation of your vision. In chapters 6 through 9, I deal with how to successfully overcome these adverse conditions and alliances and come out on top.

I can't tell you who to marry or with whom to go into business, but what I can say is that by the use of common sense and prayer, you will find the answers yourself. God will bring into your life partners that you need as you occupy and follow God's Word. The Bible gives us several examples of partnerships that will help show you how to fulfill your destiny. Prime examples are David and Jonathan; Ruth and Naomi; Shadrach, Meshach, and Abenego; David and Saul; Adam and Eve; Ruth and Boaz; and Peter and John. The Bible is a goldmine that contains the keys to life, health, wealth, and prosperity.

In conclusion, there is one other partnership I want to expound on. It is that of being in partnership with gleaners. In the book of Ruth, a gleaner, a widow, ends up marrying the richest man in town. Jewish law required that land owners not strip their fields bare, but leave some of the harvest behind for the gleaners. The gleaners were defined as the poor, the widowed, and the lepers. "When you reap the harvest of your land, do not reap to the very edges of your field or gather the gleanings of your harvest. Leave them for the poor and the alien. I am the Lord your God" (Lev. 23:22 NIV). In God's economy, nothing is wasted.

In my real estate practice, I practiced gleaning by allowing new agents to assist me by doing open houses or showing properties for me. They would do the legwork, the running around at night and on weekends, which gave me much needed time for my family and allowed me to rest. This arrangement provided an opportunity for new agents to make money and get some much-needed experience with customers. One of my agents was so adept at doing this that she was able to make the Million Dollar Club in one year.

Prayer of Agreement:

Father, as I come before You, I give thanks in advance knowing that Your Word is true. I accept the truth of Your Word that says Your promise is that You would give me the desires of my heart. I accept that Your plan for my life is already mapped out on Your greater treasure map. I give thanks that the relationships, the funds, and the resources, are already in place ready for me to call them forth into the natural realm. I agree to build my web with You as my foundation. I reinforce my radials, my partners with the fruit of the spirit with love, patience, forgiveness, understanding, and wisdom. Like the spider, I agree to not judge by appearances, and instead use the vibrations of the Spirit to detect negative forces in my life. I cast my cares upon the Christ and I use prayer and the silk of love to bind and defeat my enemies. I am a spiritual midwife. I reach out to gleaners and help them along their way. I give praise in advance knowing that weeping may endure for a night, but joy cometh in the morning. In all my getting, Father, let me get understanding and wisdom. And may I always attribute all my gains to You regardless of how high I go in life.

Exercise

1. What am I building my web upon?

2. What is my foundation?

3. Do my radials (partners) have admiral qualities?

4. Are my radials (partners) elastic? ____ yes ____ no

5. After fishing all night (John 21:3–6), have you caught anything with your "sticky silk" of love, forgiveness, patience, and endurance? ____ yes ____ no

6. Like the spider, what large prey are you binding and defeating?

7. Can my relationships endure tension?

8. What happens when I expose my partners to the light?

9. Am I able to partner with nonbelievers and those of a different race, gender, sexual orientation, or political persuasion?

10.　What have I left behind for the gleaners?

11.　Regardless of how high I go in life, do I attribute my ability to gain wealth, prestige, and fame to God? ____ yes ____ no

Chapter 6

Destroying the Yokes that Bind Us

And it shall come to pass in that day, that his burden shall be taken away from off thy shoulder, and his yoke from off thy neck, and the yoke shall be destroyed because of the anointing (Isa. 10:27).

Come unto me, all ye that labor and are heavy laden, and I will give you rest. Take my yoke upon you, and learn of me; for I am meek and lowly in heart: and ye shall find rest unto your souls. For my yoke is easy and my burden is light (Matt. 11:28–30).

Intrinsic in sales are the customary highs and lows associated with changes in the economy, seasons, interest rates, and buyers' and sellers' willingness to negotiate and consummate a transaction. Many a salesperson or business person reach a threshold where questions arise as to whether their chosen profession is their true calling.

My success in transcending this period can be attributed to three steps I used to gain dominion and overcome these challenges. I will now detail for the reader the three-step plan I used to destroy the yokes of bondage in my life. The first step was strict adherence to my Seven-Step Success Plan. The second step involved the use of the anointing of God, and the third step was the application of the Word of God. These are the steps that have been the foundation of my success.

The secular and the superficial things will be obvious to the reader in the first process, but it is typically during the second and third phases that many individuals get stuck in the unfolding of their dreams. What I will detail are the things that happen behind closed doors, when you are by yourself and your faith is low and you begin to doubt whether your chosen profession is really your calling. What follows are the spiritual principles I used to sustain me through this traumatic period in my life.

Joyce's Seven-Step Success Plan

1. Acknowledge God as the head of your life. Know who you are in Christ—that you are heir to the Abrahamic covenant (Gal. 3:13–14). Fall in love with God. Seek ye first the kingdom of God (Luke 12:22–31).

2. Give an offering and tithe 10 percent of your gross income to your church (Mal. 3:8–12). Make the tithing principle as natural as breathing. Do it without questioning!

3. Ask for spiritual armor (boldness). Encourage yourself with these verses: Know that no weapon that is formed against thee shall prosper . . . (Isa. 54:17). Learn how to stand and persevere. "Not by might, nor by power but by my spirit saith the Lord" (Zech. 4:6). "For God has not given me a spirit of fear, but of a sound mind" (2 Tim. 1:7). Understand that these things will be and *can only be* accomplished by the Spirit.

4. Call and follow through regularly and systematically on expired listings and For Sale By Owners (FSBOs). (Insert whatever prospecting techniques that are appropriate for your line of work: call past clients for leads, cold call new clients, etc.)

5. Use software to prospect and follow through with clients. Adopt the spirit of the Chaldeans and make their philosophy an intrinsic part of your philosophy (see chapter 4).

6.   Invest in your business; send sold brochures, new listing brochures, and calendars to customers, clients, and prospects. (Again, substitute whatever marketing materials are appropriate for your profession.)

7.   When you accomplish your goal, be the leper that says thanks and gives God the credit, honor, and glory!

Although I was using my Seven-Step Success Plan and my treasure map as a road map of sorts, I still encountered many obstacles prior to achieving my success in real estate. The first step in this process was not enough. It was time to move to the second and third phases of my plan by applying the anointing of God and the Word to destroy the yokes in my life. The approach to overcoming these obstacles was based on an interpretation of the following Scriptures referenced at the beginning of this chapter in Isaiah and Matthew. In order to understand how I could destroy these yokes, I think it is important to begin by defining what the term "yoke" means.

According to Webster's dictionary, "yoke" as a noun is defined as a frame fitted to a person's shoulders to carry a load in two equal portions. Other definitions include a clamp that embraces two parts to hold or unite them in position. Servitude, bondage, and tying together are also other definitions of "yoke." The word "yoke" as a verb is used to describe a joining together as in marriage. The working definition I want to emphasize is that of joining together, the uniting of two in position to accomplish a task.

Three questions, a sort of spiritual jolt, arose in me as follows: *What yokes am I trying to destroy? What darkness am I trying to dispel in my life? What task am I trying to accomplish?* I answered my own questions by recalling that God had to dispel darkness in order to create the universe. He formed a mental picture—a treasure map, if you will—and called it forth. It took six days to accomplish this and He did not rest. The Bible tells us one day is as with a thousand with God (2 Peter 3:8). If God labored to bring forth creation, why did I think that I didn't have to labor? If Jesus labored as a carpenter, why did I think that I didn't have to labor?

If God did not rest until the seventh day, why did I think I should rest before I had completed my goals? I told myself that God appointed days, times, seasons, and individuals to carry out His plan. In the natural, we have all we need to multiply and be fruitful. Remember we read in chapter 2, "of his fullness all we have received." If this is true in the natural, it follows that it must be true in the spirit realm. After all, we are told in the Word that God is Spirit. And if according to His Word we are made in His image, than we need to start acting like Him.

Like David, I had to take control and encourage myself. I did so by preaching to myself and asking the following questions: *What appointments have I made? What darkness am I commanding to be dissolved? What lights am I calling forth? What creations am I calling forth into my life? What am I saying "let there be," so that it might be? Have I made appointments to meet with a certain number of FSBOs or expired listings? Have I sent out letters to my sphere of influence? Have I signed up to take a course that will enhance my skills? Have I followed God's command to come unto Him? Have I dispelled the yokes of this world and taken on God's yoke?* He said that when I did I would find rest.

What about "His yoke allows us rest?" was my next question. Bear in mind that a yoke in the natural when placed on you, your neck, or your shoulders will cause bruising. It hurts, it causes pain. It is the fulfillment of the sweat-of-the-brow curse that Adam suffered when he was expelled from the Garden of Eden. Although a definition of yoke is to carry a load in two equal portions, this is only true in the secular world. This does not describe what happens when you take on Jesus' yoke in the spirit realm.

Although I had taken control and used fleshly attempts or my own efforts to destroy the yokes of bondage in my life, this was not enough. I had not destroyed the yokes in my life. I had to become yoked to Christ. When yoked to Christ, or when coupled with Christ, you put on spiritual armor. This brings me to the second part of my premise. It is the anointing that lightens your load. Until you put on the anointing, that spiritual armor of God, your load will be heavy.

Who are you coupled with? Who is willing to stand yoked with you to accomplish a task? Who is your partner? If it's the Anointed

One, then He is your silent partner and will be there in the fiery furnace, the lion's den, out on the sea, or wherever you are. The anointing is the unseen One, the footprints in the sand, the One who prepares a table before us in the presence of our enemies. The One who is with you always. He's the gardener when you go to the empty tomb. He's the One you need Him to be. He's the Father, the Son, and the Holy Ghost. This is when you find rest: when you stand in your yoke of bondage and know and trust that your silent partner, sweet Jesus, is there and that His promise that He would never leave you or forsake you is true. The Bible tells us that, "God is not a man that he should lie" (Num. 23:19).

When Jesus came, He declared, "The Spirit of the Lord is upon me because he has anointed me to preach the gospel . . . to set at liberty those that are bruised" (Luke 4:18). If the anointing is present, the Word will be preached and people will be set free (Isa. 10:27). The anointing must not be only on the outside, but more important, on the inner man, the spirit within, in order to be transformed by Christ.

The Bible gives us many verses of comfort demonstrating God's commitment to stand yoked with us. The Word tells us to lay aside every weight that so easily besets us and to cast our cares on the Christ and go free (Heb. 12:1; 1 Pet. 5:7). Christ will carry our burdens if we do the above. On the cross He was bruised for us. He took our weight that we might go free. He agreed to be yoked with us in order that we might be set free. Remember that He that keepeth thee "shall neither slumber nor sleep" (Ps. 121:4).

This is when I personally was set at liberty, when I rested in the Lord. This is how I overcame the yokes in my life—by calling on the name of Jesus, by casting my cares upon Him, by occupying, by standing on the Word, by standing still and knowing that God is the one true God. And when I did this, when I did all that I knew to do, that's when the silent partner, the Anointed One showed up and removed the yokes in my life through His Spirit. The Bible says "that it is not by might, nor by power, but by my Spirit saith the Lord of Hosts" (Zech. 4:6).

I want to use an example from the natural world to explain the third part of my premise, which is applying the Word of God. That is how eating of the bread of life, which is the Word of God, enabled me to destroy the yokes of bondage in my life. I must first impart to you the analogy of bruising in the formation of bread to get this point across. We know that bread sustains life and it is highly recommended as one of the essential food groups. In fact, bread is at the base of our food pyramid; it's the foundation for a healthy, long life.

Consider the following four definitions from the *Oxford American Dictionary*.

1. "Chaff" is defined as wheat husks separated from the seed by threshing or winnowing.

2. The verb "chafe" means to make or become sore from rubbing; to become irritated or impatient.

3. The next definition is "thresh." It means to beat out or separate (grain), to make violent movements.

4. The last definition is "winnow." It means to expose (grain) to a current of air by tossing or fanning it so that the loose dry outer part is blown away, to sift or separate from worthless or inferior elements.

In order to grow in the natural or spiritual, this separating from worthless or inferior elements must take place. What do you think Tiger Woods is doing when he continues to practice constantly? He's sifting and separating himself from inferior elements, those who are not willing to go the extra mile.

The process of chafing, separating the husks, is to get at the wheat germ that is the nucleus of the seed of wheat. The seed contains the vitamins. We know that from this wheat germ we are able to make bread. Therefore, from this violent process of separating and of bruising, vitamins, life's nourishment, come forth in the natural. The wheat must undergo this chafing and bruising in order to produce something that is good, something that sustains life.

Therefore, in the Spirit, be happy when you are bruised for God's sake. Know that when He sifts you, the blessings must come forth. Our part is to submit to this sifting, this winnowing. But we must do it by violent means. Matthew 11:12 puts it this way: "And from the days of John the Baptist until now the kingdom of heaven suffereth violence, and the violent take it by force." We have a part to play in separating ourselves from worthless or inferior elements that keep us in bondage. Remember that Jesus told us He was the bread of life. He was bruised for us on the cross that we might have life.

> [When the disciples] found him on the other side of the lake, they asked him, "Rabbi, when did you get here?" Jesus answered, "I tell you the truth, you are looking for me, not because you saw miraculous signs but because you ate the loaves and had your fill. Do not work for food that spoils, but for food that endures to eternal life, which the Son of Man will give you. On him God, the Father has placed his seal of approval." Then they asked him, "What must we do to do the works God requires?" Jesus answered, "The work of God is this: to believe in the one he has sent." So they asked him, "What miraculous sign then will you give that we may see it and believe you? What will you do? Our forefathers ate the manna in the desert; as it is written: 'He gave them bread from heaven to eat.'" Jesus said to them, "I tell you the truth, it is not Moses who has given you the bread from heaven, but it is my Father who gives you the true bread from heaven. For the bread of God is he who comes down from heaven and gives life to the world." "Sir," they said, "from now on give us this bread." Then Jesus declared "I am the bread of life. He who comes to me will never go hungry, and he who believes in me will never be thirsty" (John 6:25–35 NIV).

Do you see the connection I'm trying to make? If bread in the natural is at the base of the food pyramid and it is necessary to sustain life and if we take on the true Bread of Life—Jesus, the One who will stand yoked with us, who will carry our burdens and stand with us in the fiery furnace—how much more will our quality of life be enhanced? Remember, He said that He came that we might have life and that more abundantly (John 10:10). That being the case, we must demonstrate and bring into fruition what we have called forth and declared on our treasure maps. Know that the sifting and the bruising are necessary (i.e., the rejection by customers, clients, friends, or coworkers), but Jesus will see you through. Jesus will stand yoked with you and carry your burdens.

You will have to be like the apostle Paul and shake off some snakes from your life. The story of Paul on the island of Malta (Acts 28:1–10) is a fitting example. To paraphrase, Paul was helping to build a fire for warmth and a snake came out because of the heat and fastened itself to Paul's arm. The islanders initially thought that Paul must have been a murderer to have been attacked, but when he suffered no ill effects, they said he must be a god. The story ends with all the sick on the island being brought to Paul and being cured. The islanders then honored Paul and his companions "with many honours" and when they departed, they "laded" them (weighed them down) with supplies they needed.

As you progress in your calling, you will encounter many vipers, many snakes that want to stand in your way and attempt to steal your joy. Expect the criticism, expect the jealousy, and expect the rejection. All the potential customers and clients will not fall in love with you. Your peers, friends, neighbors, and family may see you as a murderer, rather than as a god, i.e., they may see you as evil and greedy, and try to discourage your good intentions.

Expect that when you put God first in your life and stand yoked with Christ, you will encounter opposition. As you attempt to get close to Christ, to get warm by His cleansing, His healing fire, some snakes are going to come out of the fire. Darkness and light cannot dwell together. The snakes have no choice but to come out and try to fasten themselves on you. They seek to destroy you, to lower your self-esteem, to bring you down to their level, to tell you that you're not good enough to excel in your profession. The Word says that God is no respecter of persons (Acts 10:34). His will is that we have life and that more abundantly. So, do like Paul did, apply the Word of God and shake off the vipers in your life.

As a side note, in all my eighteen years of selling real estate, only one client ever threatened to take me to the Real Estate Commission. It is no coincidence that when I experienced this challenge to my license, it was not from a stranger but as a result of the actions of my dad in a real estate transaction with me as the selling broker. My silent response to my dad telling me that I could move to another state and open another company was, "though you slay me yet shall I serve you." In other words, "though you bruise me, I shall yet serve God, because he's sifting me for a higher purpose."

At this point, I hope I have opened your spiritual eyes. It is a revelation to me, and I hope you see the connection between this and the pursuit of your vocation. As I have given to my agents and to you, the reader, I minister to myself. Sometimes I feel I'm ministering more to myself than to you. By my pouring out these words, I feel a healing. I know I'm addressing it to you on one level, but on another level, I also feel compelled to share this with myself alone. I experience a satisfaction and strengthening that's hard to explain.

As I decrease and allow God to increase, as I eat of His Word (i.e., the true bread of life) and apply the Word, I become a manifestation of the Word. As I take His yoke upon me, He brings continuous prosperity into my life. In 2001, we added twelve agents to Rainbow Realty. In 2002, we added an additional eleven agents. It's not me, it's not my husband, and it's not by our powers . . . it's by the Holy Spirit that we are enjoying success and prosperity. It is the anointing that breaks the yokes and makes the difference. When God awakens me at night and shares these truths, I have no other choice but to pass them on to others. I hope you can receive them, as I have received and been enlightened. I hope you don't see it as foolishness but as truth to the point that it sets you free to accomplish your heart's desires and be the head and not the tail!

Prayer of Agreement:

Let us come into agreement now as a corporate body . . . those who wish and are able may join hands as a symbol of the joining together of our hearts and minds . . . demonstrating our willingness to stand yoked with one another in the Spirit and with Jesus, the Christ.

    Father, we come boldly together in the name of Jesus Christ of Nazareth and declare that no weapon formed against us shall prosper. We come together corporately and agree that we shall, we will, put God first in our lives. We renew the commitment we made that by putting God first, He would grant our desire to become life members of the Million Dollar Club [or whatever accomplishment you are trying to achieve].

    In the name of Jesus the Christ, we shake off poverty, unbelief, discouragement, and tiredness. We shake off weariness and greed. We shake off the desire for too many foods that give us a quick high, and for too many fatty foods. We shake off all the things that weigh us down and attempt to ensnare us and replace them with good eating habits, not only in the natural, but more important, in the spiritual.

    We desire now to take from the tree of life and eat the true bread of life. We call forth patience, persistence, love, forgiveness, obedience, joy, enthusiasm, longsuffering, and faith. And, Father, when we receive our Million Dollar Club plaque [or whatever recognition or designation is appropriate for your profession], *we commit now that we will be like the one leper who comes back and gives God the glory for bringing these desires into fruition. In Jesus' name we give thanks, this or something better, Father. Let your unlimited good will be done!*

Exercise

1. Are you yoked with the Christ, is He your silent partner?   ___ yes ___ no
2. Are you becoming bruised for Christ in the process of realizing your dream(s)?   ___ yes ___ no
3. Are you using the anointing oil of Jesus, the oil of forgiveness, patience, love, and humility (i.e., the fruits of the Spirit) to destroy the yokes in your life?   ___ yes ___ no

4. Are you passing up foods that don't sustain
   life and rob you of your energy and are
   destructive to your physical body?   ___ yes ___ no

5. Are you eating the true bread of life or
   nibbling on crumbs one day a week on
   Sunday morning?   ___ yes ___ no

6. Have you shaken off anything that keeps you
   separated from the Christ—poverty, sickness,
   alcoholism, drug addiction, hatred, selfishness,
   jealousy, covetousness, weariness, homosexuality,
   fornication, adultery, or unbelief?   ___ yes ___ no

7. Have you done all you know to do and now
   you stand, waiting, knowing that it's the
   anointing that will destroy the yokes of
   bondage by the Spirit of God?   ___ yes ___ no

8. Are you becoming the manifested Word
   by applying the Word of God to your life?   ___ yes ___ no

Chapter 7

The Weapon of Forgiveness

After Job had prayed for his friends, the Lord made him prosperous again and gave him twice as much as he had before (Job 42:10 NIV).

Envy thou not the oppressor, and choose none of his ways (Prov. 3:31).

. . . and they shall rule over their oppressors (Isa. 14:2).

And he said unto me, My grace is sufficient for thee: for my strength is made perfect in weakness. Most gladly therefore will I rather glory in my infirmities, that the power of Christ may rest upon me (2 Cor. 12:9).

The material that follows in this chapter is an outgrowth from one of my company's sales meetings in which I did a motivational segment on how forgiveness played a key role in bringing into fruition the desires on my treasure map.

It is important to first define the terms "weapon" and "forgiveness." What is a weapon? The *American Heritage Dictionary* defines it as "any instrument used in combat" or "any means employed to get the better of another." An example the dictionary gives of this second definition is, "Her smile was her most effective weapon."

What definition is given for the word "forgive"? It is as follows: "to excuse for a fault or offense; to pardon; to renounce anger or resentment against." Another definition is "to absolve from payment of; to grant pardon without harboring resentment." The definition God uses is a superlative one; it is of the highest nature. When He forgives us, He forgets the offense. It is like it never happened. It is because He forgets that we are free to enjoy the fullness of life if we would only reach out and grab hold of it.

I want to illustrate the effectiveness of forgiveness by sharing two well-known biblical examples. In the Old Testament, the weapon of forgiveness played a part in the last chapter of Job in bringing about restoration, abundance, and a healthy, long life in the physical realm. In chapter 6, I dealt with destroying the yokes that bind us by eating and partaking of the true bread of life. In this chapter, I would like to focus on the importance of destroying yokes in the natural, but more important, in the spiritual. I want you to see how forgiveness played a part in destroying Job's yoke, and how the breaking of bread brought about a restoration to Job and his family and freed him to enjoy the true bread of life in the spirit realm.

> Then Job replied to the LORD: "I know that you can do all things; no plan of yours can be thwarted. You asked, 'Who is this that obscures my counsel without knowledge?' Surely I spoke of things I did not understand, things too wonderful for me to know. You said, 'Listen now, and I will speak; I will question you, and you shall answer me.' My ears had heard of you but now my eyes have seen you. Therefore I despise myself and repent in dust and ashes." After the LORD had said these things to Job, he said to Eliphaz the Temanite, "I am angry with you and your two friends, because you have not spoken of me what is right, as my servant Job has. So now take seven bulls and seven rams and go to my servant Job and sacrifice a burnt offering for yourselves. My servant Job will pray for you, and I will accept his prayer and not deal with you according to your folly. You have not spoken of me what is right, as my servant Job has." So Eliphaz the Temanite, Bildad the Shuhite and Zophar the Naamathite did what the LORD told them; and the LORD accepted Job's prayer. After Job had prayed for his friends, the LORD made him prosperous again and gave him twice as much as he had before (Job 42:1–10 NIV).

Then came there unto him all his brethen, and all his sisters, and all they that had been of his acquaintance before, and did eat bread with him in his house: and they bemoaned him, and comforted him over all the evil that the LORD had brought upon him: every man also gave him a piece of money, and every one an earring of gold. So the LORD blessed the latter end of Job more than his beginning: for he had fourteen thousand sheep, and six thousand camels, and a thousand yoke of oxen, and a thousand she asses. He had also seven sons and three daughters. And he called the name of the first, Jemima; and the name of the second, Kezia; and the name of the third, Kerenhappuch. And in all the land were no women found so fair as the daughters of Job: and their father gave them inheritance among their brethen. After this lived Job an hundred and forty years, and saw his sons, and his sons' sons, even four generations. So Job died, being old and full of days (Job 42:11–17).

Similarly in the New Testament, but of far more reaching consequences for all humanity, forgiveness played a part in bringing about a harvest in the life of Jesus for all believers through His forgiveness of His enemies after He [the bread of life] was broken [bruised] on the cross. Jesus uttered these famous words, "Father, forgive them; for they know not what they do" (Luke 23:34). After His resurrection it is important to note what happened at the breaking of bread in Luke 24:30–31. It reads as follows: "And it came to pass, as he sat at meat with them, he took bread, and blessed it, and brake, and gave to them. And their eyes were opened, and they knew him; and he vanished out of their sight."

And at the discussion of the breaking of bread in (Luke 24:35–36): "And they told what things were done in the way, and how he was known of them in the breaking of bread. And as they thus spake, Jesus himself stood in the midst of them, and saith unto them, 'Peace be unto you.'" Jesus again and again attempts to tell us that He is the true bread of life. Likewise when we eat of His bread (i.e., die to self like Jesus did), come together in His name in unity, practice forgiveness, accept Jesus' blood as atonement for our sins, and drink the wine of the New Testament which is being filled with the Holy Ghost, then we become endued with power. *It is then that Jesus shows up in the midst.*

As we partake of Him, Jesus appears to us and we become flesh of His flesh and bone of His bone. As partakers, as sons and daughters, we become heirs not only to eternal life, but heirs to the abundant life on earth as expressed in Mark 10:29–30: "And Jesus answered and said, 'verily I say unto you, there is no man that hath left house, or brethren, or sisters, or father, or mother, or wife, or children, or lands, for my sake, and the gospel's, But he shall receive an hundredfold now in this time, houses, and brethren, and sisters, and mothers, and children, and lands, with persecutions [with bruising of the flesh]; and in the world to come eternal life.'"

After Jesus' resurrection He appeared to the disciples and other followers. Jesus told them in Luke 24:46–53:

> And [He] said unto them. Thus it is written, and thus it behoved Christ to suffer, and to rise from the dead the third day: And that repentance and remission of sins should be preached in his name among all nations, beginning at Jerusalem. And ye are witnesses of these things. And behold, I send the promise of my Father upon you: but tarry ye in the city of Jerusalem [place of praise], until ye be endued with power from on high. And he led them out as far as to Bethany, and he lifted up his hands, and blessed them. And it came to pass, while he blessed them, he was parted from them, and carried up into heaven. And they worshipped him, and returned to Jerusalem with great joy: And were continually in the temple, praising and blessing God. Amen.

What were Jesus' followers instructed to do? Plain and simple. He said practice forgiveness; tell all nations about me; white people, black people, red people, yellow people; people you don't like; and, in particular, your enemies. Eat of me, partake of my crucifixion [my bruising], of my bread, my Word, be a witness of me and tarry in Jerusalem, in that place of praising and blessing God and I will send you the promise of the Holy Spirit which will endow you with all power. When you receive the promise, you will boldly say, No weapon formed against me shall prosper; if God be for me, who can be against me; I can do all things through Christ who strengthens me; I am the head and not the tail!

What does this mean to you and me? For myself, it means that if I want God's blessings, His prosperity, His health, if I want to be a Million Dollar Club member, if I want to leave an inheritance that can be passed down from generation to generation like Job, then I must forgive my enemies completely, wholly, and take of the true bread of life, and stay in the atmosphere of Jerusalem (i.e., stay in a place of praising God). When we do this, Jesus will appear to us, yokes of bondage will be destroyed, and Jesus will give us the desires of our hearts.

I would like to say from personal experience that I have tried the practice of forgiveness and, beyond a shadow of a doubt, it works! Without hesitating, I can say that this is a strong and powerful arsenal of warfare that works in mysterious and wonderful ways. One Scripture in particular honed in on my spiritual psyche in my teens without me having a full understanding of its meaning, and it has stuck to my spirit to this day. It is found in Proverbs 3:31 and reads, "Envy thou not the oppressor, and choose none of his ways." As a black Christian teen in the 1960s, in a world of stark contradictions, the impression it made on me was mind boggling. In spite of the gross inequities in the world, and towards blacks in particular, I was told that I was supposed to love and forgive those who had and continued to oppress me. This did not sit well with me, but in my spirit I knew the Word was right. I reasoned that it was better to obey God than man, so I committed to love and forgive all my enemies.

I pressed on in life and attempted as best I could to love my enemies. Four years after graduate school I relocated to Atlanta. One of the Job-like experiences I faced occurred while I was single and had just bought a new townhouse and a new car. I had no family in Atlanta and had decided to leave the profession of social work and branch out into real estate sales full time. I left behind me a ten-year career as a social work supervisor, a master's degree from Simmons College in Boston, Massachusetts, and a twenty-one-thousand-dollar annual income. I felt I was going nowhere fast.

The handwriting was on the wall. The social work agency could not contain me. Like Jonah, they wanted me out of the boat. They knew I was different. I guess I was too black, too female, not willing to be a "good girl" and play by their rules. They did not know that I was secretly selling real estate part-time. Those within the agency became jealous when they saw my new red car and my new townhouse that God had blessed me with through my faith in Him and my commitment to giving tithes and offerings.

After selling ten houses while working full time as a social work supervisor, I decided it was time for me to jump ship before they spewed me out. Working full time in real estate soon became a challenge that turned into a burden. I did not have a business plan. I did not understand how to plan my activities or secure prospects so that I could have a consistent income on which I could depend.

I made only eight thousand dollars in my first year in the real estate business. I called home and my sister told me that I was living too fast, buying both a new car and a new house, and it had finally caught up to me. She told my dad not to lend me any money because I wouldn't pay him back. Although she gave me $33.33 and my dad lent me a small amount of money above the going interest rate (which, by the way, I did pay back), I was still broke. I suffered the embarrassment of going to the bank to cash a check for $33.33. What could I buy with thirty-three cents? The bank teller could see that I had next to nothing in the bank. So I continued to charge my mortgage and pay other bills by living off of cash-advance checks from credit card companies. My prayer to God at this point was *Please, no more credit cards, no more cash advance checks, no more contracts that don't close, no more listings of unsaleable homes.* I needed real money that could only come from real closings.

At this point in my life I experienced a health challenge that made me realize that I had to stop working three jobs. I accepted in my mind and in my heart that real estate was what I wanted to do even if I didn't get paid for doing it. I accepted that I could do it and do it well, and that it was only a matter of time before I would be successful. I accepted in my mind that I might have to sacrifice some things like my townhouse, but it would be worth it. I would be back; it was just a matter of time.

I made up my mind that I needed to put God to the test or, should I say, put *myself* to the test to see if I would be able to trust

God. The issue was whether or not I would continue to praise Him, continue to put Him first in my life, continue to teach Sunday school, and to give tithes and offerings from the little I had. I accepted that in spite of everything, God loved me, and that it was His will that I have life and that more abundantly. More important, I came to the realization that it was not by my might, nor by my power, but by God's Spirit that my success in real estate would be accomplished.

Like Job, I had to stop pleading my case and work on forgiving my enemies, my friends, my family members, and myself. I had to work on forgiving buyers who were not truthful or loyal after I had shown them several homes; sellers who were demanding, rude, or who wanted to cut me out of a commission; my prayer partner who told me to give up the idea of selling real estate and stopped praying with me; and my family who gave me just enough to say they helped, but so little that it was not enough to do anything substantial with. *In spite of the wrongs that were committed against me, I had to reject the ways of my oppressors, and choose God's excellent way of love and forgiveness.*

And when I did, the most glorious, mind-freeing, life-changing thing happened. I realized that God's Word is true; that you can't beat what God gives us; that His will is truly that we have life and that more abundantly. I went from making eight thousand dollars my first year full-time (using the arm of flesh) to making forty-two thousand dollars the second year (using God's more excellent way). God had multiplied my income more than five times and doubled what I made as a social worker with a master's degree from a prestigious New England college and ten years' work experience.

Looking back, who would have thought that in 2001, the little colored girl from the projects would be forty-eight years young, married, have a six-year-old, and co-own a real estate company on a main thoroughfare in a suburb of Atlanta, Georgia with twenty-five agents? You can't tell me God is not good. The blessings that He has for us if we believe are more than what we can ever think of or imagine. And guess what? It doesn't stop there, it keeps getting better!

Prayer of Agreement:

Let us now close our eyes and relax our minds and come into agreement as a corporate body that we will reach out in spirit now and forgive our enemies, whoever they may be. We release and let go of anger, disappointment, unbelief, tiredness, weariness, greed, hurts, and falsehoods that wear us down and attempt to destroy us. We choose none of the ways of our oppressors, and choose God's more excellent way of love and forgiveness. We substitute faith, love, kindness, mercy, and forgiveness. We forget those things that lie behind (there is no way we can change the past) and we press towards the high mark which is in Christ Jesus who holds the promise of abundant life, health, prosperity, and wisdom. In Jesus' name, we give thanks and say together, thank you, Father; thank you, Father; thank you, Father; and so it is.

Exercise

1. I now forgive myself for not living up to my full potential. I forgive myself for harboring unkind thoughts or for any unkind acts I have committed against _____.
   I take personal responsibility for my thoughts and actions.

2. I now forgive the following persons for any offenses, real or perceived, committed against me: _____

3. Like Job I stop pleading my case and forgive my enemies named: _____

4. I also forgive those enemies that are lodged within the "inner me" named: _____

5. I send out a blanket of forgiveness into the universe for any offenses of which I may not be aware.

6. I partake of Jesus' crucifixion, of His bruising of the flesh by dying to any of the following that hinders my spiritual development and progress:

___ jealousy	___ drug addiction
___ envy	___ sexual perversions
___ covetousness	___ fornication
___ anger	___ adultery
___ overeating	___ alcoholism
___ lasciviousness	___ greed
___ fear	___ hate
	___ unforgiveness

_____ other(s)

7. I choose God's more excellent way and I practice and demonstrate in my life the fruits of the spirit as follows:

___ love	___ goodness
___ joy	___ faith
___ peace	___ meekness
___ long-suffering	___ temperance
___ gentleness	

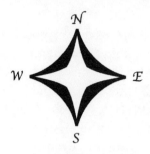

Chapter 8

The Weapon of Giving

And being in Bethany in the house of Simon the leper, as he sat at meat, there came a woman having an alabaster box of ointment of spikenard very precious; and she brake the box, and poured it on his [Jesus'] head (Mark 14:3).

Why do some people give offerings or tithes and still don't experience success or prosperity? Why do some people work hard at a goal but never see it materialize, or never get the promotion they feel they deserve? I have found throughout my life that giving or the lack of giving can expedite or impede the flow of blessings in our lives. In this chapter I will answer these questions and explain a system of giving that unfailingly will create abundance in your life because it is based on the system that Jesus called the more excellent way.

Let me qualify this first by saying that in your quest for obtaining a six-figure income, don't become so obsessed with the fish and loaves that you miss out on the greater riches that God has in store for you. Remember Jesus said to "seek ye first the kingdom of God and his righteousness and all these things shall be added" (Matt. 6:25–34). You seek the Kingdom of God by giving the alabaster gift that goes beyond the giving of tithes and offerings.

81

Before I describe the more excellent way, I'll share the concept of tithing in relation to obtaining a six-figure income.

In her book, *The Millionaires of Genesis*, Catherine Ponder explains how, through the use of the tithing principle, Adam, Abraham, Melchizedek, Isaac, Jacob, Joseph, and Ruth became millionaires. Giving of the tithe, 10 percent of your gross salary, derives from the Old Testament covenant of giving a tenth back to God (Gen.14:17–20). The tithe is spiritually based. It has to do with dying to self, obeying God's commandment, and remaining in covenant with God. The tithe in the Old Testament symbolized dying to self; the offering was actually burnt, it suffered a death and was killed (Exod. 13:11–13; Lev. 27:28–30).

In the New Testament, Jesus told us that, "unless a kernel of wheat falls to the ground and dies, it remains only a single seed. But if it dies, it produces many seeds" (John 12:24 NIV). Jesus became God's tithe. Because Jesus was clean and without sin, He was offered up as the sacrificial lamb. Through this act, mankind has been redeemed and we are thus able to come before God in a clean and righteous manner. And since Jesus is now our High Priest after the order of Melchizedek (Heb. 4:14–5:10), we in turn give our tithes and offerings to the source of our spiritual supply. This is typically our local church (Heb. 7:1–5, 1 Cor. 16:1–3).

Perhaps this concept of tithing can best be understood in the natural by Ponder's explanation that "if the farmer refused to give back to the soil a certain percentage of the crops [seeds] which the soil had given to him, he would have no crops." If this is true in the natural, then it follows that if we want to be supernaturally blessed, than we must follow God's spiritual laws which are supernatural. We must give back a portion of our increase, die to some things, so that we might have some crops, some increase in our lives. The supernatural quality of the tithe is that it is the first fruit, the best. God gave His best, His first fruit, when He gave His only son, Jesus. The Bible says in Romans 11:16, "For if the first fruit be holy, the lump is also holy: and if the root be holy, so are the branches." Herein lies the magic of the tithe. If the first fruit is blessed, consequently the remainder is also blessed and prospered.

God's promise concerning the giving of tithes and offerings in the Old Testament in Malachi 3:8–12 is that He would throw open the floodgates of heaven and pour us out such a blessing that we would not have room to contain it. His promise is that it would be so great that all nations would call us blessed. While this commandment is important, in 1 Corinthians 12:31, Paul tells us to seek the more excellent way of charity, as demonstrated by the sinful woman who anointed Jesus' feet with the alabaster box of expensive ointment in Mark 14:3. Another account is given presumably of this same woman in Luke. Jesus said to Simon and the Pharisees of her:

> "Seest thou this woman? I entered into thine house, thou gavest me no water for my feet, but she hath washed my feet with tears, and wiped them with the hairs of her head. Thou gavest me no kiss: but this woman since the time I came in hath not ceased to kiss my feet. My head with oil thou didst not anoint: but this woman hath anointed my feet with ointment. Wherefore I say unto thee, Her sins, which are many, are forgiven; for she loved much . . ." (Luke 7:44–48).

The tithe and the offering are the fulfilling of the law, "this ye ought to do" (Luke 11:42), but the alabaster gift is of the heart. It is the more excellent way, it is not of the law. Everything that is the more excellent way is of the heart; it cannot be *taught*, it is *caught*. And because it is a gift, it comes from within and happens when an individual comes to themselves like this woman and pours out and breaks under the anointing (at the foot of Jesus) that which is most precious and gives it to God. This woman was restored completely and made whole. Her spiritual conscious was that of a baby's—free and pure. And with this type of cleansing she was free to begin again. She was loosed to be all that she dreamed or desired to be—the guilt, shame, insecurities, and sense of unworthiness were forgiven and forgotten. She was free to begin again.

From a psychological point of view, any therapist will tell you that one of the main reasons why many of their patients can't be made whole is because they can't forgive themselves, or that they can't let go of the past. Nor can they forgive the abusers of their past, so they stay stuck in an emotional time zone. They tithe, they come to church, but their dreams aren't fulfilled. Their basic needs for the most part are met—they have food, clothing, and shelter (God rains on the just and the unjust). But their innermost dreams and a sense of wholeness are not fulfilled.

The questions that must be asked and answered for each of us include: *What is most precious to me? What do I need to give to God? What addictive behavior holds me in bondage that I need to release at the foot of Jesus? Is it addiction to drugs, sex, money, fame, negative emotions, or people?* The alabaster gift is when you give all; it's when you pour out your heart without expecting to get something back in exchange.

The woman with the alabaster box gave her all; she gave beyond the tithe and the offering. The equivalent she gave was more than a year's salary. How many of us would give more than a year's salary without the expectation of getting something in return? This woman gave all she had without expecting something in return. If we give a tithe and offering and God opens the floodgates of heaven, how much more will He give us if we, like the sinful woman, give the alabaster gift of love to God?

Put another way, Jesus said in Mark 10:29–30, "There is no man that hath left house, or brethren, or sisters, or father, or mother, or wife, or children, or lands, for my sake, and the gospel's. But he shall receive an hundredfold now in this time, houses, and brethren, and sisters, and mothers, and children, and lands, with persecutions; and in the world to come eternal life."

When Ruth forsook all and left her family behind to follow Naomi's God of the Israelites, she ended up marrying Boaz. She became not only a millionaire but also an ancestor of Jesus. Rahab the prostitute, by aiding the spies and forsaking her family and social group, married and became an ancestor of Boaz, David, and Jesus. Abraham made preparations to sacrifice his son, forsook the best land of the Jordan, and instead chose peace and brotherhood. God gave him and his offspring in return all the land he could see forever, i.e., all that he in his mind attempted to conquer. Genesis 22:18 prophesied of Abraham the following: "Your descendants will take possession of the cities of their enemies, and through your offspring all nations on earth will be blessed, because you have obeyed me" (NIV). Joseph, forsaken by his brothers, ends up being second in authority only to the pharaoh. Job forsook his wife and the pleasures of this world and received a double portion of all he formerly possessed. Jesus forsook the kingdoms of this world and now sits at the right hand of God, constantly making intercession for us so that we might receive eternal life and never thirst again for any good thing while we are here on earth.

Don't seek for an exchange on what you give to God. He knows the fish and the loaves that you need. You must trust that when you obey and practice righteousness, which is "right thinking," all things shall be added. This is God's promise; He doesn't lie. It is automatic. All things must be added, so don't worry. God will and must fulfill His part of the covenant. If your exchange is obedience, then you, too, as a seed of Abraham, are automatically entitled to become a millionaire like Abraham, Ruth, Joseph, and others who chose to seek first the kingdom of God and His righteousness.

God's commandment to seek Him first seems so simple, and I think that because it is so simple, the wise of this world are confounded by it. Many of my accomplishments were derived from simple acts of stepping out on faith, obeying God's Word, giving of tithes and offerings, and putting God to the test that He would bless according to his Word.

Prayer of Agreement:

Having accepted Jesus as my personal savior, I make a commitment to be obedient to His Word. I accept and give thanks that I am of the seed, of the loins of Abraham by faith. Like Adam, Abraham, Melchizedek, Isaac, Jacob, Joseph, and Ruth, I commit to be a tither and a giver of offerings. I strive to be like the woman with the alabaster box and give that which is most precious to me and surrender (brake) it before Christ. Whatever I have made as an idol—be it money, clothing, houses, children, my spouse, sex, prestige, fame, my body, my business, my way of thinking, and any other offenses known or unknown to me—I agree to surrender and lay them at the foot of the Christ. I cast my cares on the Christ and go free.

Exercise

1.   I acknowledge that I am obeying God's Word according to Malachi 3:8 and have made the commitment to freely and lovingly give of my tithes and offerings. ___ yes ___ no

2.   I make this commitment without expecting something in return. This is not an exchange for something of value that I hope to receive at some future date. I give out of love and go beyond the fulfilling of the law, by giving of whatever is in my alabaster box. I lay at Jesus' feet whatever is most precious to me. I make a commitment that if God never blesses me with the desires of my heart, I will faithfully serve, love, worship, and trust in Him because I am consciously seeking Jesus and not things. ___ yes ___ no

3.   The following things:

    ___ money   ___ gods

    ___ cultural fixations   ___ belief systems

    ___ dreams   ___ persons

are most precious to me. Like my predecessors [Abraham, Job, Isaac, Ruth, Joseph, the woman with the alabaster box], I now release and commit them to God.

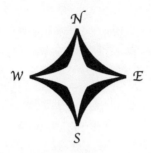

Chapter 9

The Weapon of Praise

And when they began to sing and to praise, the LORD set ambushments against the children of Ammon, Moab, and Mount Seir, which were come against Judah; and they were smitten (2 Chron. 20:22).

And they were continually in the temple, praising and blessing God . . . (Luke 24:53).

In chapter 7, I shared with you how the weapon of forgiveness played a key role in the lives of Job, Jesus, and myself. I delineated how Job, a prosperous man, received double of all he previously had after praying for and forgiving his enemies. I talked about how Jesus forgave us and gave His life for us so that we might have abundant life here on earth and in the life to come. I also shared with you my personal experiences of forgiveness of my family and friends and living off of credit cards to pay my bills. I then explained how, after enduring these crises, I cofounded with my husband a successful real estate firm in metro Atlanta.

In this chapter, I want to focus on how the weapon of praise was used to develop and foster prosperous relationships and promotions in my life. I received the gift of the Holy Ghost as a teenager after "tarrying" for it at Christ Temple Church of Personal Experience in the Roxbury section of Boston, Massachusetts. This was accomplished by simply praising God, asking for forgiveness, asking Jesus to fill me with the Holy Ghost, and waiting for the manifestation.

In the Old Testament, God sent an ambush to destroy the enemy while the Israelites were praising God. But in the New Testament He gave us His Holy Spirit to empower us to destroy the enemy through the use of praise and speaking the Word. In Mark 11:23–25 and Romans 4:16–17, we are told as the seed of Abraham through faith, we can call into existence that which we desire. We can even go as far as to call dead things back to life and remove all mountains and all obstacles in our lives.

The gift of the Holy Ghost comes from the Father, who promised to send us the Comforter to assist us in our daily walk through life's vicissitudes (Luke 24:49; Acts 1:8). Because our sins have been redeemed by the shedding of Jesus' blood on Calvary, we are able to receive a spiritual transfusion, or an adoption into the family of Christ. We consequently have become joint heirs with Jesus. The power to destroy all manner of sickness, disease, debt, and demonic forces is given to us by the receipt of the Holy Ghost. The blood of Jesus, His Spirit, is able to cleanse us and make us whole. It has sustaining power and is able to keep us whole.

Interestingly enough, perhaps, this transformation can be understood by a dream I awoke to on August 20, 2003. As a confirmation of this truth, in the dream, I saw a man who said that he had a blood transfusion and had not experienced any problems since the transfusion because it was good blood. Likewise, in the spirit realm, it behooves us to have a spiritual transfusion, because Jesus' blood is able to cancel all manner of sickness, pain, and demonic forces in the natural and in the spiritual.

By this adoption we now have the blood of Christ running through our spiritual veins. We are made clean and whole because His Spirit gives us sustaining power. We can now plead the blood over situations in our life and know that the creative force, the same authority who made heaven and earth, is within us. It waits for us to speak it into existence. The Word says that God is able to keep that which is within us until the day of redemption (2 Tim. 1:12).

My life has not been the same since the receipt of the Holy Ghost some thirty years ago. I didn't see stars, but I do remember a bright light, experiencing acceptance, forgiveness, and God's Spirit moving through my body. I'm sorry for those of you who believe that you have to speak in tongues in order to receive the Holy Ghost. I didn't. But I did receive His Spirit, and I have no doubt that He moves in and flows through me. And I did receive the gift of wisdom, the gift of faith, the gift of teaching, and the gift of love. The Bible says that we would not all speak in tongues, but that love was the more excellent way and that this should be our pursuit, to love Him first and our neighbor as ourselves (1 Cor. 12:4–13; 1 Cor. 12:31–13:1, 13:13; Matt. 22:36–40).

Some of the blessings and miracles I have received throughout my life include a four-year scholarship to a private, suburban high school outside of Boston, free private piano lessons, healing of a broken toe and skin disease, a four-year scholarship to Simmons College in Boston, a two-year scholarship to Simmons College Graduate School of Social Work, a beautiful son David, houses, and a trip to Germany as an ambassador with the Friendship Force. The list goes on and on. This is pretty impressive stuff for a kid from a dysfunctional family who grew up in one of Boston's inner-city projects.

However, I was not welcomed by Boston public schools due to segregation. What seemed on the appearance to be a terrible injustice turned out to be one of the best things that could ever have happened to me. At Palfrey High School, I was free to excel and compete with other students who represented various religious backgrounds and whose parents had old and new money. Palfrey was like a little United Nations that attempted to do its share during the 1970s of making Dr. Martin Luther King's dream a reality, that all men and women could live together in love and brotherhood and enjoy a prosperous life. What I experienced during those four years at Palfrey was a sense of entitlement. Not only did I learn with the affluent, but I also played and partied with the affluent. Unfortunately, at the end of high school, I was still a black girl from the inner city of Boston.

After receiving my undergraduate and graduate degrees, I was able to find employment in my chosen profession. But I was still haunted by what I had experienced at Palfrey High School. I liked, but did not covet, the freedom and luxury of money. I was attracted to being able to go on a ski vacation whenever I wanted or the freedom to choose fresh juice, fruit, and cream cheese and bagels for breakfast rather than just a bowl of corn flakes.

After moving to Atlanta in 1980, I heard the teachings of Dr. Barbara King-Blake at Hillside Chapel and Truth Center and of the late Doctor Arlene Williams (a minister who in 1982 was in charge of a $25-million plan of operation in Chicago) on prosperity. Reverend Williams's message was empowering because it told me that it was fine to be born again, filled with the Holy Ghost, college educated, and have money and lots of it! I learned from her of my spiritual entitlement that as a seed of Abraham, I could have the desires of my heart. I learned that I could move mountains and destroy yokes of bondage.

What Dr. Arlene (as she was affectionately called) stressed, however, was that after all the whooping and hollering was over (i.e., praising God), one needed to have a plan of attack to call forth total prosperity in your life. That plan included obeying God's Word; giving of tithes, time, talent, and offering to the Church; having a vision and speaking it forth into existence by way of words; and most important, a plan and corresponding action. Faith without works is dead (James 2:26). God's charge to us in Genesis 1:28 is to be fruitful, multiply, and take dominion over world systems.

Dr. Arlene had made her money in the dry-cleaning business. In 1982, her church covered over a city block in Chicago. This was somewhat of a stretch from real estate, but the business principles and applications she gave were close enough that I could garner some underlying truths and apply them to my situation.

I received another revelation of the importance of praise through a tape by Bishop T. D. Jakes of Texas called "The Sacrifice of Praise." This message hit home after the death of my stillborn daughter and bored into my subconscious mind and my spirit that the victory of Jericho, of David, was in praise *in spite of* one's circumstances. I learned through application and experience that if you want the goodness and mercy of God, then you must make a joyful noise, serve the Lord with gladness, come before His presence with singing, and be thankful unto God as pictured in Psalms 100.

The beautiful and refreshing thing about doing it God's more excellent way (1 Cor. 12:31, 13:13) of following his Word, of exercising love, is that He meets all of your desires. The prosperity that God gives is not like what some of my associates from Palfrey High School had; based on stocks, steel, degrees, or old money. Instead, this kind of prosperity is based on God's Abrahamic promise that wherever you place your feet (your desire, your understanding), you shall have victory in the form of all the money you need, health resources, good relationships, and peace of mind. But the caveat is that we must put God first and then all things are added.

This is not a denial of the need to invest in stocks, education, or the world's economy. But your foundation must be in Christ, who will reveal all things to you in the fullness of time. What I want to underscore is that when you seek God first and receive the Holy Ghost, all things are added; but we must be in a state of preparedness, of occupying until He comes so that we don't have to spend so much time trying to make up for lost time. Let me emphasize that I believe the reason I received scholarships to a private high school, a private undergraduate and graduate school, and other blessings was because I was in a state of readiness, of occupying. When I received a scholarship to a private high school, I was not looking for it. I was studying and getting As and Bs at my ghetto school and my gift made room for me. Proverbs 18:16 reads, "A man's gift maketh room for him, and bringeth him before great men."

We must do like Daniel and commit to excellence and domination of world systems, so that we can inherit and possess the land. If you have never taken a course on aeronautics, how can you fly a plane? How do you know whether or not you should buy an airline and what type of workers you should hire? How can the government be upon our shoulders if we know nothing of world history, global economics, world trade, world geopolitics, the environment, different religions and belief systems, or how to delegate authority? Training is essential. Knowledge of world systems is essential. How can you overcome the world without an understanding of how it works? You must be superior like the secular Chaldeans were in their time as mentioned in chapter 4. Faith without works is dead!

Prayer of Agreement:

Precious Father, I come before You with an open and receptive mind and spirit. I ask for Your forgiveness and acknowledge that I am a sinner. Father, You said in John 3:16 that if any man ask for forgiveness and salvation that You would grant it to them. I ask now, Father, that You would save me and grant me eternal life. I accept now, Father, that You have answered my prayer, because You said that Your will is that no man would perish. I rejoice now and accept Your gift of salvation through Your son Jesus Christ. I give You praise, honor, and glory! I vow to worship You from this point with my whole heart. Father, I believe; help my unbelief.

Exercise

Once you have accepted Jesus Christ as your personal savior, He promises to send the Comforter, which is the Holy Ghost, to empower us to overcome all adversities in life (John 14:12–27). Not only does the Holy Ghost allow us to tread on serpents (negative forces), but He gives us the gifts of the Spirit—wisdom, knowledge, faith, healing, working of miracles, prophecy, and speaking in tongues (1 Cor. 12:8–13). These spiritual gifts applied to our life are like icing on a cake; they make our way safe, successful, and prosperous! Through these gifts we are empowered to destroy all yokes, bind the enemy, and overcome all challenges to truly be the head and not the tail.

If you have not received the Holy Ghost, I would implore you to align yourself with a church, a fellowship of believers who demonstrate maturity in the Spirit and believe in tarrying for the Holy Ghost. I dare you to ask Jesus to fill you with the Holy Ghost. The gifts of the Lord are without repentance (Rom. 11:29–36). If you have received the gift already and have let it lie dormant, then ask the Father for a revival of His Spirit in you. You really don't know what you are missing! You may think your life is sweet now, but with the application of the Holy Ghost you will add a sweetness to your life that will give you a sugar high that is indescribable. The ways of the Lord are sweeter than the honeycomb and in keeping them there is *great reward* (Ps. 19:7–11).

Once we have received the gift of the Holy Ghost, it is important to take the next step and begin from our experiences to press forth the fruit of the Spirit. We must desire the more excellent way, to give the gift of the alabaster box as mentioned in chapter 8. The gifts of the Spirit are what God gives to us, but the fruit of the Spirit—love, joy, peace, long-suffering, gentleness, goodness, faith, meekness, and temperance (Gal. 5:22)—are what we give back to demonstrate to the world that we belong to Christ because we have taken on His nature.

Chapter 10

How to Pass on Generational Wealth

And when these lepers came to the uttermost part of the camp, they went into one tent, and did eat and drink, and carried thence silver, and gold, and raiment, *and went and hid it*; and came again, and entered into another tent, and *carried thence also, and went and hid it* (2 Kings 7:8).

She considereth a field, and buyeth it: with the fruit of her hands she planteth a vineyard . . . She perceiveth that her merchandise is good: her candle goeth not out by night . . . She stretcheth out her hand to the poor, yea she reacheth forth her hands to the needy (Prov. 31:16–20).

My focus in this final chapter is on how to pass on generational wealth to your family, that is, how to enter another tent and hide some things for your children's children. Put another way, I want to share with you how you can enter another level of consciousness so that you can launch yourself and your family to a higher level. If you have made a decision to make six figures, then I would urge you to take the next step, which I feel inspired to share with you. It is a message that has been burning within me and it is taken from 2 Kings 7 and Matthew 25.

Parenthetically, one of my agents who had seen the marquee outside my office which read, "I press to be nearer to thee in 2003" questioned whether this was a church or a real estate office. My response was yes, this is a real estate office. But if you get the concept of seeking God first and understand the totality of what Jesus meant by this, then there would be no lack of any good thing in your life. The houses, the husbands, the wives, Million-Dollar-Club status, the six-figure income, all the resources that you need, including health, would be yours. So to reiterate, I told my inquisitive agent this is a real estate office and yes, I try to carry the church within me, within my workplace. I try not to keep it on the shelf during the week and take it down only on Sundays like a special hat.

I ask the reader to use spiritual ears even though you may have read or heard a message preached on these passages of Scripture before. I ask that you not judge, but listen with your heart, for I believe that God has given me this message for a reason. I believe it is a message that is designed to break the yoke of bondage and set you free, that you may conquer all the giants in your life. I can say with all certainty that it has and does continue to destroy the yokes in my life.

The passages are as follows:

And there were four leprous men at the entering in of the gate: and they said one to another, Why sit we here until we die? If we say, We will enter into the city, then the famine is in the city, and we shall die there: and if we sit still here, we die also. Now therefore come, and let us fall unto the host of the Syrians: if they save us alive, we shall live; and if they kill us, we shall but die. And they rose up in the twilight, to go unto the camp of the Syrians: and when they were come to the uttermost part of the camp of Syria, behold, there was no man there. For the LORD had made the host of the Syrians to hear a noise of chariots, and a noise of horses, even the noise of a great host: and they said one to another, Lo, the king of Israel hath hired against us the kings of the Hittites, and the kings of the Egyptians, to come upon us. Wherefore they arose and fled in the twilight, and left their tents, and their horses, and their asses, even the camp as it was, and fled for their life. And when these lepers came to the uttermost part of the camp, they went into one tent, and did eat and drink, and carried thence silver, and gold, and raiment, and went and hid it; and came again, and entered into another tent, and carried thence also, and went and hid it. Then they said one to another, We do not well: this day is a day of good tidings, and we hold our peace: if we tarry till the morning light, some mischief will come upon us: now therefore come, that we may go and tell the king's household (2 Kings 7:3–9).

For the kingdom of heaven is as a man traveling into a far country, who called his own servants, and delivered unto them his goods. And unto one he gave five talents, to another two, and to another one; to every man according to his several ability; and straightway took his journey. Then he that had received the five talents went and traded with the same, and made them other five talents. And likewise he that had received two, he also gained other two. But he that had received one went and digged in the earth, and hid his lord's money. After a long time the lord of those servants cometh, and reckoneth with them. And so he that had received five talents came and brought other five talents, saying, Lord, thou deliveredst unto me five talents: behold, I have gained beside them five talents more. His lord said unto him, Well done, thou good and faithful servant: thou hast been faithful over a few things, I will make thee ruler over many things: enter thou into the joy of thy lord. He also that had received two talents came and said, Lord, thou deliveredst unto me two talents: behold, I have gained two other talents beside them. His lord said unto him, Well done, good and faithful servant; thou hast been faithful over a few things, I will make thee ruler over many things: enter thou into the joy of thy lord. Then he which had received the one talent came and said, Lord, I knew thee that thou art an hard man, reaping where thou hast not sown, and gathering where thou hast not strawed: And I was afraid, and went and hid thy talent in the earth: lo, there thou hast that is thine. His lord answered and said unto him, Thou wicked and slothful servant, thou knewest that I reap where I sowed not, and gather where I have not strawed: Thou oughtest therefore to have put my money to the exchangers, and then at my coming I should have received mine own with usury. Take therefore the talent from him, and give it unto him which hath ten talents. For unto every one that hath shall be given, and he shall have abundance: but from him that hath not shall be taken away even that which he hath. And cast ye the unprofitable servant into outer darkness: there shall be weeping and gnashing of teeth (Matt. 25:14–31).

I would like to offer my interpretation as follows. Four lepers are at the entrance of the city gate in a time of famine. Who are these four men who are lepers? What do they signify? According to the law, lepers were contagious and were not allowed in the city. They would beg for food or wait for scraps to be thrown over the city wall. Because of the famine, these men decided to press in, knowing that either way they would die, but chose to at least risk getting some food rather than to stay outside the city, do nothing, and die anyway.

Who are the modern-day lepers that are told to stay back? They are, as I see them today, oftentimes women, people of color, the uneducated, the poor, the diseased, and those with HIV/AIDS. The modern-day lepers have many faces and, in one form or another, often include ourselves. We face a famine of sorts every day in our lives. We wake up and hear the bad news—layoffs, termination, cut backs in benefits, uncertainty about the future and quality of our lives. These are the bruised individuals of society that Jesus came to set at liberty (Luke 4:18). These are the uncircumcised that Jesus spoke about (Rom. 4:12; Acts 10:45). They are the unclean individuals that *Peter was admonished by the Lord to include in the body of Christ* (Acts 10:28, 34–35).

We, like the lepers, need to rise up at twilight, when things are dark and gloomy, when our backs are up against the wall, and have enough faith to say, "If I'm going to die, let me die trying to get some food, rather than doing nothing." I believe that when we stand still—after we have done all we know to do—surrender our cares to God and acknowledge our human limitations, then God will fight our battles. It is then that He causes our enemies to flee. According to 2 Kings 7, when the lepers saw that the Syrians had deserted the camp, the lepers went into a tent, ate and drank, and then they carried off silver, gold, and clothing, and hid them.

What jumps out at me is how they reacted when they came into abundance. They made a decision to hide their wealth. You see, once their physical needs had been taken care of, they realized they were still lepers, so they hid their wealth. We—as lepers, as women, as people of color, as whatever we claim our leprous, bruised condition to be—must learn like the lepers to hide our wealth. You see, they realized that after the famine was past, as lepers, they would still be mistreated and would need food, clothing, and shelter to protect against the elements.

What are we as modern-day lepers doing with our silver and gold? Are we investing it so that our children's children will have wealth? Like the lepers, we are not able to change our gender, color, background, the stock market, inflation, or world economics, but we can make investments today that will affect our retirement and our children's grandchildren's future.

I hope you can hear with your spiritual ears what I am trying to convey. Gold has always been accepted universally as a measure of wealth and medium of exchange to buy goods. The silver is what you use to buy what you need today (food and clothing); but the gold is for tomorrow's investment. The point is not to bury your gold as the servant did in the parable of the talents but to be like the servants that had two or five talents, invested them, and multiplied the gifts they had. Or as my mother would say, "they used what they had." They used the natural gifts that God gave them.

God expects us to prosper. He expects us to take what we have and multiply it. A faithful servant will take whatever he has, bless it, and multiply it. Dorothy found out in *The Wizard of Oz* that her ability to go home, to excel in life, was within her. We likewise must realize that we have to click our heels and search vigilantly like Dorothy. We must speak the Word and become doers of it and *work* while it is still day, because the darkness will come and no man can work (John 9:4). We watch and pray, but we *work*; we stand still and see the salvation of God, but we *work*.

The *American Heritage Dictionary* defines "work" as "physical or mental effort or activity directed toward the production or accomplishment of something; toil; labor; employment; a job; the means by which one earns one's livelihood; a trade, craft or profession, to make productive, cultivate, to function or operate in, to persuade, influence or affect." Please note there is no reference to playing the lottery, gambling, using company time to do personal errands, marrying a wealthy person, or wishing or hoping for a miracle. Also of importance are the varying definitions of work. Work does not necessarily connote drudgery. Work, when you are in your anointing, can be child's play because you are doing what you enjoy doing. It does, however, require time, effort, and energy.

Another pitfall we as Christians often succumb to is becoming super religious. We think that if we just pray long enough, loud enough, or cry out before God, our prayers will be answered. The Bible says to watch and pray, which means while we are occupied (working, walking uprightly before God, trusting Him, obeying God's Word, giving of our tithes, talents, and offerings), God will command a blessing and all yokes will be removed.

In fact, the servant who took his one talent and hid it in the ground was called a wicked and slothful servant. The master told him he should have at least put the one talent in the bank and should have drawn interest on it. It has always amazed me as to why the master took the wicked servant's one talent and gave it to the servant that had ten talents. I understand now that it is because God is serious about us being fruitful and multiplying (*working*) the talents He has given to us. The Bible does not tell us to be leeches but to be fruitful and multiply. God did not create this marvelous universe for us to cry, "I'm poor and broke." God is not the author of poverty, sickness, or disease. He is the author of super abundance and His children must be like their father and demonstrate super abundance and prosperity in all arenas of life.

How can we spread the gospel throughout the world with limited funds or if we are in poor health? How can we be the head without funds to put governments under our authority? How can we send our children to the best schools without funds? How can we ensure our grandchildren's children don't live a life of poverty? How can we be purveyors of quality housing for all Americans?

One way we can invest our gold is through real estate. Real estate is a commodity that is exhaustible. Everyone needs someplace to lay his or her head at night. Most millionaires have used real estate to establish or launch their economic footing. My dad, who didn't graduate from high school, unknowingly prompted me to go into real estate when I saw how the triplex he bought in Boston, Massachusetts, for fourteen thousand dollars provided an ongoing cash flow and retirement income for my parents.

In the past twenty years of selling real estate, I have learned a lot from my customers and clients. Surprisingly, I have learned more from my salt-of-the-earth clients than the supposedly more enlightened and educated consumers. We live in a credit-oriented society. Those individuals who mismanage their finances are over-consumers and, simply put, do not pay their bills on time, often pay a heavy cost. I have seen many salt-of-the-earth individuals living on small salaries amass fortunes in real estate. They start a small portfolio by buying one small property that they live in and then move on and acquire additional properties.

They are not following the advice of some real estate guru, but they simply use common sense, invest sweat equity, and live within their means. They use what they have, they occupy, and when the opportunity arises to buy additional properties, they jump on it. They are able to do so because they have paid their bills on time, lived within their means, and thus slowly built a handsome real estate portfolio.

Real estate agents, in particular, should be amassing large port-folios of properties. They are in the front lines and usually receive the first call when an owner wants to move. The seller may be moti-vated to move due to job relocation, need for a larger or smaller home, or pending foreclosure or bankruptcy, divorce, or job layoff. Those agents who have set aside funds (their gold) have first pick-ings and should ask themselves, *Is this property one that I can buy, fix up if necessary, and rent out and hold for retirement?* Location is impor-tant and does determine value and appreciation. But remember Walt Disney amassed his fortune using swamp land. Keep in mind, they're not making any more land, and with the right idea and plan, even a deserted, poverty-stricken area can be turned around and made profitable.

Another benefit of buying property is that realtors, individuals, or organizations (including churches), can provide quality housing for others who are credit challenged. This allows families to get out of roach- and rat-infested developments and prosper. It is hard for a child to dream and hope for a better life if his or her environment is infiltrated with drug dealers, poverty, and immoral and illegal activities. Cooperative projects using government money can be embarked upon by individuals or churches to turn houses into Section 8 homes, halfway houses, maternity homes, or treatment centers. Obtaining real estate gives you collateral and leverage, which enables you to develop more lucrative projects. It is simply a matter of what the mind can conceive.

For owner-occupants and first-time buyers, there are several legitimate no-money-down programs that are available to prospective homeowners. There is virtually no reason why anyone should not own a home who is working in America. For those who are credit challenged, there are legitimate agencies that will help you repair your credit for free.

Returning to 2 Kings 7:9, the following statement was made by the lepers: "We are not doing right. This day is a day of good news, if we are silent and wait until the morning light, punishment will over take us; now therefore come, let us go and tell the king's household." What good is it if you make it into the land of abundance, of light, and your brothers and sisters are still in darkness?

You see, I feel that as I have been freed from a situation of famine in my own life, I must go and share the good news with the body of Christ, the King's household. I feel that it is crucial that I share how God enabled me to achieve Million-Dollar-Club status now going on my twelfth year. This book is my attempt to give you a clear idea and a step-by-step plan on how you can take your dreams, regardless of your profession, and manifest them into a six-figure income and leave an inheritance to your children.

The book *The Millionaire Next Door* is an excellent resource and companion to this book, but it leaves out the spiritual component. What good is it if we gain the whole world, if we learn how to invest the gold, but we lose our souls? This earth, although we are mandated by God to possess and dominate it, will be left behind when we die. We must take our example from the caterpillar on how to live life. I believe God has fashioned the metamorphosis of the caterpillar into a butterfly to give us a peek into what eternity will be like.

I walk early in the morning and I am amazed at how many caterpillars there are and that they eke out such a lowly existence. They are everywhere, and their lives seem so fragile. It is extremely difficult to avoid stepping on them. Their lives can be extinguished in a second, but yet they persist and many live to become marvelously radiant-colored butterflies. The caterpillar seems to have such faith. It doesn't worry that it might not live another day. It enjoys life with a strong will to live and appears fearless.

But the incredible thing about the caterpillar is the miraculous transformation it makes into a butterfly. How is it that something that crawls around on the ground all its life can die to its old self and emerge as a radiant creature with wings and look down on its tormentors of the past? Is this not a demonstration in the natural of the tail becoming the head? If God will do it for the caterpillar, won't He do it for us, His highest form of creation?

Likewise in the spirit realm, we must leave an inheritance to our children so that they don't perish in eternity. What good is it if our children are able to speak four or five different languages and become rulers of this world, amass fortunes in real estate and other holdings, but perish in eternity like the caterpillar? My Bible says that only what you do for Christ will last and that with all your getting, get understanding. It says to get wisdom, which is the principal thing.

And so to you, the reader, I proclaim upon you in the name of Jesus Christ of Nazareth, that the blessings of Abraham are upon you. May you use your gold to take dominion over all that you tread upon through Christ Jesus in this world, but also more important, use your gold to give birth to the caterpillars, to the bruised of this world, and foster their evolvement into butterflies in heaven.

We who are gifted, blessed, and have been able to navigate through this economic system and the spiritual chaos that abounds, must become spiritual midwives and usher in others. We must leave some behind for the gleaners as in the book of Ruth—so that a Ruth, a Naomi, a Boaz, a David, a Jesus may evolve into a butterfly and transcend the constraints of this world. Hebrews 12:12–13 (NIV) puts it this way, "Therefore strengthen your feeble arms and weak knees. Make level paths for your feet, so that the lame may not be disabled, *but rather healed.*" We who are spiritual midwives must not get weary in our well doing, but must raise our arms in praise in spite of our circumstances. We must fight the good fight of faith regardless of how we feel, and strengthen our knees and walk on. We make our paths level by understanding that the battle is not ours but the Lord's, and He will deliver us. And when we do this, then we are able to empower the lame of this world to be healed.

Dr. Martin Luther King Jr. had a dream; I also have a dream. My vision is that the church would usher in the promise of the Father, that new kingdom where there will be no crying or dying and we can sit at God's feet and be blessed. Godspeed.

Prayer of Agreement:

God said in His Word that He would take the simple things of this world to confound the wise. Right now I want you to lay aside your preconceived notions about what the world has told you about success. We are going to become like children and do these simple or foolish things right now. I'm warning you that I may offend some of you or make you feel uncomfortable. But I can only give you what I know and share with you what I have done over the years. As David said, I can't put on someone else's armor. This is my armor, albeit spiritual, that I committed to share with you regarding my success.

If you are ready, then I ask that you demonstrate this by joining your hearts with me (since there is no separation or distance in spirit) and, if you can, join your hands together with a partner, friend, or loved one as we come into agreement as one collective body making our petition before God.

Father, in the name of Jesus, You said in Your Word that if two or three would come together as one, that You would be there in the midst thereof. You said to ask, and it shall be done. Father, we come together as one, agreeing that we are the seed of Abraham and that we are joint heirs of Your kingdom. We have decided to put You first in our lives, to give You the first fruits of our monies, time, and talents. We commit to break our alabaster box before You and if You never bless us with anything else, we commit to remain loyal and serve You with a heart of gladness. We commit to seek You and not material things, knowing that, as a loving Father, Your delight is to bless Your children and to give us the desires of our hearts, also knowing that Your promise is that You would never forsake us.

Father, we ask now that You would make us the head and not the tail by teaching and instructing us how to do what the head does. Help us Father to manifest the fruit of the Spirit—love, peace, joy, patience, kindness, goodness, faithfulness, gentleness, and self-control—like You, Father, because You are the head. Help us Father to become doers of Your Word.

Father, You said in Your Word that we must speak the Word and call it forth. You said that we have not, because we ask not. In the name of Jesus Christ of Nazareth, we ask that You would rain down _____ (insert that which you need in order to prosper and be in good health).

If you are real estate agents, ask for saleable listings, binding contracts, and abundant closings. If you are in the cleaning business, ask for skill, precision, patience, and abundant cleaning contracts. An attorney would ask for skill, wisdom, and the ability to articulate and pontificate settlements in a client's favor. An artist would ask for creativity and clarity so that his or her paintings would sell and receive acclaim; a painter would ask for referrals to paint other houses. A surgeon would ask for discernment, skill, and tenacity for successful medical outcomes. A minister would ask that souls would be saved and filled with the Holy Ghost, followed by a permanent change in the individual's inappropriate behavior. A baker would ask for creativity, flavorful recipes, and abundant orders.

Now you must say it and believe it. If you believe it, call it forth now for yourself. You have everything to gain. Let us say it together with a loud voice. Let your enemies of doubt and disbelief scatter and run off. Let those enemies of fear flee from you. Fear is nothing but false evidence appearing as real. What is real is that you are sons and daughters of the Most High; we are the head and not the tail.

(Author's example) *Listings, contracts, and closings come to me now listings, contracts, and closings come to me now listings, contracts, and closings come to me now.* _____ (Substitute what is appropriate for your profession.)

    Father, we accept that You have heard and answered our petition. Now we run on and act as if it is already done. We rejoice and commit to spread the good news of the gospel with others. The good news of forgiveness, love, deliverance, healing, reconciliation, peace, prosperity, and wisdom. Amen.

Exercise

1.   I am using my talent(s) as follows:

2.   I am investing my gold as follows:

3.   I am making the transformation to a butterfly because I am dying to the following things:

___ greed	___ hatred
___ jealousy	___ envy
___ insensitivity	___ proscrastination
___ unforgiveness	___ unkindness
___ fear of dying	___ fear of failure
___ fear of success	___ fear of people
___ fear of tomorrow	___ fear of the unknown
___ lack of self-confidence	___ selfishness
___ other _____	___ sexual perversion

4.   Do we as Christians see modern-day lepers—the dispossessed, society's downtrodden, homosexuals, the underclass, HIV carriers—as contagious? ___ yes ___ no

5. Do we shun them? ___ yes ___ no

6. Are we willing to physically touch them? ___ yes ___ no

7. Are we willing to eat with them or be seen with the socially downtrodden? ___ yes ___ no

8. I help the body of Christ by doing the following things:

9. I am becoming a spiritual midwife by doing the following things:

10. I accept I am becoming the head because I am doing what the head does: I practice love, forgiveness, and peace with all. I go the extra mile when no one sees what I am doing. I am a tither and I give of what's in my alabaster box. I have given my life to Christ and am filled with the Holy Ghost. I am bold and fearless. I love Jesus, and I spend time with Him daily. I eat right, exercise, and take care of my body temple. I listen to God's still voice and I respect authority. I teach my children and those under me the ways of the Lord by my words, and more significant, by my actions. I make investments in this world, but more important, I make investments in God's kingdom. Until Jesus' return, I commit to use my God-given talents and I am occupying the earth. I am working and taking dominion of the earth. I am multiplying the gifts God has given me. I am heaven bound, but I am of earthly good. The love of Jesus in me attracts others to the Christ within them. I am a fisher of men and women for the kingdom of Christ Jesus. Since God is for me, who can be against me! I've read the end of the book (Revelation); it says that we win! All praise goes to God Almighty!

APPENDIX

Rainbow Realty Company Theme Songs

I'm Blessed, I'm Blessed!

Verse 1:   I'm blessed, I'm blessed, I'm blessed.
I am bless–ed.
I have shelter, clothing, health, and strength; and I'm bless–ed.
I'm blessed, I'm blessed, I'm blessed.
I am bless–ed.
I am a child of God and I'm blessed.

Verse 2:   You're blessed, you're blessed, you're blessed.
You are bless–ed.
You have shelter, clothing, health, and strength; and
   you're bless–ed.
You're blessed, you're blessed, you're blessed.
You are bless–ed.
You are a child of God and you're blessed.

Verse 3:   We're blessed, we're blessed, we're blessed.
We are bless–ed.
We have shelter, clothing, health, and strength; and
   we're bless–ed.
We're blessed, we're blessed, we're blessed.
We are bless–ed.
We are children of God and we're blessed.

Verse 4:   I'm blessed, I'm blessed, I'm blessed.
I am bless–ed.

I have listings and contracts that close on time and
   I'm bless-ed.
I'm blessed, I'm blessed, I'm blessed.
I am bless-ed.
I am a child of God and I'm blessed.

Verse 5:   You're blessed, you're blessed, you're blessed.
You are bless-ed.
You have listings and contracts that close on time and
   you're bless-ed.
You're blessed, you're blessed, you're blessed.
You are bless-ed.
You are a child of God and you're blessed.

Verse 6:   We're blessed, we're blessed, we're blessed.
We are bless-ed.
We have listings and contracts that close on time and
   we're bless-ed.
We're blessed, we're blessed, we're blessed.
We are bless-ed.
We are children of God and we're blessed.

(Author unknown—modified version)

Happy Am I, I'm Rich, I'm Happy

Verse 1:   Happy am I, I'm rich, I'm happy;
Happy am I, I'm rich today;
Happy am I, I'm rich, I'm happy;
Happy am I, I'm rich today.

Verse 2:   Oh, happy am I, happy am I,
Oh, happy am I, happy am I,
Oh, happy am I, happy am I,
I'm rich today.
(now point to your neighbor)

Verse 3:   Happy are you, you're rich, you're happy;
            Happy are you, you're rich today;
            Happy are you, you're rich, you're happy;
            Happy are you, you're rich today.

Verse 4:   Oh, happy are you, happy are you,
            Oh, happy are you, happy are you,
            Oh, happy are you, happy are you,
            You're rich today.
            (now point to everyone)

Verse 5:   Happy are we, we're rich, we're happy;
            Happy are we, we're rich today;
            Happy are we, we're rich, we're happy;
            Happy are we, we're rich today.

Verse 6:   Oh, happy are we, happy are we,
            Oh, happy are we, happy are we,
            Oh, happy are we, happy are we,
            We're rich today.

                                    (Author unknown)

Bibliography

Bailey, Jill. *How Spiders Make Their Webs (Nature's Mysteries)*. New York: Benchmark Books, 1997.

Ehrlich, Eugene H. *Oxford American Dictionary*. New York: Oxford University Press, 1980.

MacDougall, Mary Katherine. *What Treasure Mapping Can Do For You*. Unity Village, Mich.: Unity School of Christianity, 1968.

Morris, William, ed. *The American Heritage Dictionary of the English Language (New College Edition)*. Boston: Houghton Mifflin Co., 1976.

Murphy, Joseph. *Telepsychics: The Magic Power of Perfect Living*. West Nyack, N.Y.: Parker Publishing Co., 1973.

Ponder, Catherine. *The Millionaires of Genesis: Their Prosperity Secrets for You!* Camarillo, Calif.: DeVorss & Company, 1979.

Stanley, Thomas J. and William D. Danko. *The Millionaire Next Door: The Surprising Secrets of America's Wealthy*. Atlanta: Longstreet Press, 1996.

Webster's New Dictionary of the English Language. New York: Popular Publishing Co., 2001.

About the Author

Growing up in the inner city of Boston, Massachusetts, C. Joyce Farrar-Rosemon didn't dream of being a successful businesswoman who would one day earn a six-figure income. Instead, after earning bachelor degrees in both psychology and elementary education and receiving her master's in psychiatric social work, she began a successful career in counseling and social work. After ten years, Joyce realized the Lord had other plans for her, and that her true calling was in real estate.

While leaving social work for a full-time real estate career was difficult (in her first year, she earned only eight thousand dollars), Joyce relied on biblical truth and the Lord's promises to guide her. She mapped out what she now calls her "Seven-Step Success Plan," became a life member of the Atlanta Board of Realtors' Million Dollar Club (an honor given to realtors who have sales in excess of $1 million for multiple years), and began living as the head, not the tail, as promised in the book of Deuteronomy.

Within a few years, she'd married, started a family, and developed what was to become one of Atlanta's most successful real estate firms. Today, that firm, Rainbow Realty Services, Inc., continues to impact lives, not only of customers and clients, but also of individuals striving to become successful entrepeneurs.

C. Joyce Farrar-Rosemon, ABR, CRB, CRS, GRI, and her husband, Tillmon H. Rosemon Jr., live in Stockbridge, Georgia. They have one son, David.

For information about Joyce's speaking engagements or empowerment seminars, or for real estate assistance, go to www.howtobethehead.com.